KEY TEXTS

T0158675

THOEMMES

Printed and bound by
Antony Rowe Ltd., Chippenham, Wiltshire

KEY TEXTS
Classic Studies in the History of Ideas

RELIGION AND PHILOSOPHY

R. G. Collingwood

THOEMMES
PRESS

This edition published by Thoemmes Press, 1997

Thoemmes Press
11 Great George Street
Bristol BS1 5RR
England

ISBN 1 85506 317 4

This is a reprint from the 1916 edition

second impression

Publisher's Note

PREFACE

IT was my intention to write this book as an essay in philosophy, addressed in the first instance to philosophers. But the force of circumstances has to some extent modified that plan. To make of it an academic treatise, armed at all points against the criticism of the professed specialist, would require time far beyond the few years I have spent upon it. The claims of a " temporary " occupation, very different from that in which I began to write, leave no opportunity for the rewriting and careful revision which such a work demands, and I had set it aside to await a period of greater leisure. But the last year has seen a considerable output of books treating of religion from a philosophic or intellectual rather than either a dogmatic or a devotional point of view ; and I believe that this activity corresponds to a widespread reawakening of interest in that aspect of religion among persons not specially trained in technical philosophy or theology. In the hope of making some small contribution to this movement, I venture to publish this book as it stands.

No one can be more conscious than myself of its shortcomings ; that they are not far greater is largely due to the patience with which certain friends, especially E. F. Carritt, F. A. Cockin, and S. G. Scott have read and criticised in detail successive versions of the manuscript.   It must not be supposed, however, that they are in agreement with all my views.

69 Church Street, Kensington, W.,
July 30, 1916.

CONTENTS

PART I

THE GENERAL NATURE OF RELIGION

CHAPTER I

1. The intellectual element in all Religion (creed). Anti-intellectual theories of Religion :—
   (*a*) Religion as Ritual.
   (*b*) Religion as Conduct.
   (*c*) Religion as Feeling.
2. Identity of creed with Theology.
3. Identity of creed with Philosophy :—
   (*a*) Negation of a special Philosophy of Religion.
   (*b*) Identity of Religion and Philosophy.
   (*c*) The supposed irreligious elements in Science.

CHAPTER II

1. The existence of a practical content in all Religion. Contradictory views :—
   (*a*) An historical argument.
   (*b*) An anthropological argument.
   (*c*) Religious determinism.
   (*d*) Antinomianism.
   (*e*) Quietism.

CHAPTER III

PART II

RELIGION AND METAPHYSICS

CHAPTER I

CONTENTS

CHAPTER II

CHAPTER III

PART III

FROM METAPHYSICS TO THEOLOGY

CHAPTER I

CHAPTER II

CHAPTER III

INTRODUCTION

This book is the result of an attempt to treat the Christian creed not as dogma but as a critical solution of a philosophical problem. Christianity, in other words, is approached as a philosophy, and its various doctrines are regarded as varying aspects of a single idea which, according to the language in which it is expressed, may be called a metaphysic, an ethic, or a theology.

This attempt has been made so often already that no apology is needed for making it again. Every modern philosophy has found in Christianity, consciously or unconsciously, the touchstone by which to test its power of explanation. And conversely, Christian theology has always required the help of current philosophy in stating and expounding its doctrines. It is only when philosophy is at a standstill that the rewriting of theology can, for a time, cease.

But before embarking on the main argument it seemed desirable to ask whether such an argument is really necessary: whether it is right to treat Christianity as a philosophy at all, or whether such a treatment, so far from being the right one, really misses the centre and heart of the matter. Is religion really a philosophy? May it not be that the philosophy which we find associated with Christianity (and the same applies to Buddhism or Mohammedanism) is not Christianity itself but an alien growth, the projection into religion of the philosophy of those who have tried to understand it?

According to this view, religion is itself no function
of the intellect, and has nothing to do with philosophy.
It is a matter of temperament, of imagination, of emotion,
of conduct, of anything but thought.   If this view is
right, religion will still be a fit and necessary object of
philosophic study ; but that study will be placed on
quite a different footing.   For if Christianity is a
philosophy, every Christian must be, within the limits
of his power, a philosopher : by trying to understand
he advances in religion, and by intellectual sloth his
religion loses force and freshness.   Above all, if
Christianity is a philosophy, it makes a vital difference
whether it is true; whether it is a philosophy which will
stand criticism and can face other philosophies on the
field of controversy.

On the other hand, if religion is a matter of temperament, then there are no Christian truths to state or to
criticise : what the religious man must cultivate is not
intellectual clearness, but simply his idiosyncrasy of
temperament ; and what he must avoid is not looseness
of thought and carelessness of the truth, but anything
which may dispel the charmed atmosphere of his
devotions.   If Christianity is a dream, the philosopher
may indeed study it, but he must tread lightly and
forbear to publish the results of his inquiry, lest he
destroy the very thing he is studying.   And for the
plain religious man to philosophise on his own religion
is suicide.   How can the subtleties of temperament and
atmosphere survive the white light of philosophical
criticism ?

It is clearly of the utmost importance to answer this
question.   If religion already partakes of the nature of
philosophy, then to philosophise upon it is to advance
in it, even if, as often happens, philosophy brings doubt
in its train.   He knows little of his own religion who
fears losing his soul in order to find it.   But if religion
is not concerned with truth, then to learn the truth
about religion, to philosophise upon it, is no part of a

religious man's duties. It is a purely professional task, the work of the theologian or the philosopher.

These issues have been raised in the First Part of this book, and it may be well to anticipate in outline the conclusions there advanced.

In the first place, religion is undoubtedly an affair of the intellect, a philosophical activity. Its very centre and foundation is creed, and every creed is a view of the universe, a theory of man and the world, a theory of God. If we examine primitive religions, we shall find, as we should expect, that their views of the universe are primitive ; but none the less they *are* views of the universe. They may be rudimentary philosophies, but they are philosophies.

Secondly, religion is not, as philosophy is generally supposed to be, an activity of the "mere" intellect. It involves not only belief but conduct, and conduct governed by ideals or moral conduct. Religion is a system of morality just as much as a system of philosophical doctrines. Here, again, systems vary : the savage expresses a savage morality in his religion, but it is a morality; the civilised man's religion, as he becomes more civilised, purges itself of savage elements and expresses ideals which are not yet revealed to the savage.

Thirdly, the creed of religion finds utterance not only in philosophy but in history. The beliefs of a Christian concern not only the eternal nature of God and man, but certain definite events in the past and the future. Are these a true part of religion at all ? could not a man deny all the historical clauses in the Creed and still be in the deepest sense a perfect Christian ? or be a true Moslem while denying that Mohammed ever lived ? The answer given in Chapter III. is that no such distinction can be drawn. Philosophy and history, the eternal and the temporal, are not irrelevant to one another. It may be that certain historical beliefs have in the past been, or are now, considered essential to orthodoxy when in fact they are not, and are even untrue ; but we cannot jump from this fact to the general statement that history is irrelevant to religion, any more than we can jump from the fact that certain metaphysical errors may have been taught as orthodox, to the statement that metaphysics and religion have nothing in common.

A fourth question that ought to be raised concerns the relation between religion and art. The metaphorical or poetical form which is so universal a characteristic of religious literature seems at first sight worlds removed from theology's prose or the "grey in grey" of philosophy. Is the distinction between religion and theology really that between poetry and prose, metaphorical and literal expression? And if so, which is the higher form and the most adequately expressive of the truth ?

To deal with these questions we must enter at length into the nature of poetry and prose, literal and metaphorical expression, and the general philosophy of language. And having raised the problem, I must ask the reader's pardon for failing to deal with it. The existence of the problem must be noticed ; but its complexity and difficulty are so great that it was found impossible to treat it within the limits of a single chapter. I have accordingly omitted any detailed treatment of these questions, and can only add that I hope to make good the deficiency in a future volume.

Philosophy, morality, art and history do not exhaust all the sides of human life, because no list of faculties or activities can ever, in the nature of the case, be exhaustive. They are taken as typical ; and if each is found to be necessary to religion, it is perhaps not very rash to conclude that whatever others exist are equally essential. Thus religion is not the activity of one faculty alone, but a combined activity of all elements in the mind. Is it, then, a true unity ? Must we not say, "Philosophy I know, and history I know, but religion seems to be merely a confused name for a combination of activities, each of which is really distinct and separate"? Does not religion dissolve into its component elements and disappear ?

No ; because the elements will not dissolve. They contain in themselves the power of natural attraction which forbids us ever to effect the separation. Or rather, each by its own internal necessity generates all the others, and cannot exist as a concrete thing till that necessity has run its course. And religion is a concrete thing, a life, an activity, not a mere faculty; and therefore it must consist of all at once. So far from religion decomposing into its elements, every individual element expands into a concrete fulness in which it becomes religion.

"Then is there no other life than religion ?" So it would appear. Just as every man has some working theory of the world which is his philosophy, some system of ideals which rule his conduct, so every one has to some degree that unified life of all the faculties which is a religion. He may be unconscious of it, just as every man is unconscious of having a philosophy before he understands what the word means, and takes the trouble to discover it ; and it may be a good or a bad religion, just as a man's system of conduct may be a good or bad morality. But the thing, in some form, is necessarily and always there ; and even the psychological accompaniments of religion—though they must never be mistaken for religion itself—the feeling of awe and devotion, of trust in powers greater than oneself, of loyalty to an invisible world, are by no means confined to persons gifted with the "religious temperament."

"But at least," it will be replied, "that is not the way we use the word ; and you can't alter the usage of words to suit your own convenience." I am afraid we cannot escape the difficulty by any method so simple as recourse to the dictionary. The question is not what words we use, but what we mean by them. We apply the term religion to certain types of consciousness, and not to others, because we see in the one type certain characteristics which in the others we suppose to be absent.   Further investigation shows that the characteristic marks of religion, the marks in virtue of which we applied the term, are really present in the others also, though in a form which at first evaded recognition. To refuse to extend the term on the ground that you have never done so before is as if one should say, " I mean by a swan a bird that is white ; to describe this black bird as a swan is merely abusing language."

We must make up our minds what we really do mean by religion ; and if we choose to define it superficially, by the colour of its feathers instead of by its comparative anatomy, we must renounce the attempt to philosophise about it, or to preach it, or to put our whole trust in it ; because none of these things can decently apply to superficialities.   But if we really try to discover what is the inward heart and essence of the thing we call religion, we must not be alarmed if we find that our practised vision sees it in places where, till now, we had not expected to find it.

PART I

THE GENERAL NATURE OF RELIGION

CHAPTER I

RELIGION AND PHILOSOPHY

To determine the relation in which religion stands to the other activities of the mind, philosophy, conduct, and so on, might seem impossible without previously defining both religion itself and the other activities or forms of consciousness. But we cannot frame a definition until we have investigated these relations ; and to offer it dogmatically at the outset would be to beg the very question we wish to solve. This is a difficulty common to all philosophical, and indeed in the last resort to all other investigations. No science is really in a position to define its subject-matter until it has brought its discoveries to a close.

Consequently we offer no definition of religion at the beginning, but hope to arrive at one in the course of our inquiry. In fact, these introductory chapters are intended to lead to a general conception of religion ; abstract indeed, because its content will only be examined in the latter part of this book, but sufficient for the purpose of preliminary definition. We start here with only one presupposition : namely, that the form of consciousness called religion really does exist. What it is, and of what it is the consciousness, are questions we shall try to answer in the course of our inquiry.

1. The first relation to be examined is that between religion and the intellect, that activity of the mind by which we think and know. The question before us is whether religion involves this activity or not ; whether

or not the intellect has a part in the religious life.   At
present we do not ask whether it constitutes the whole
of religion, and whether religion contains also non-
intellectual elements.   We only wish to determine
whether it has an intellectual element ; and if so, what
is the general nature of this element.

This question naturally leads us to investigate certain
views of religion which place its essence in something
other than thought, and exclude that faculty from the
definition of the religious consciousness.   It has, for
instance, been held that religion consists in the per-
formance of ritual acts, and that all else is secondary
and irrelevant ; or that it is neither more nor less than
a system of practice or morals ; or again that it is a
function of a mental faculty neither intellectual nor
moral, known as feeling.   We shall examine these
views as mere types, in the abstract, not criticising
any particular exposition of them, but rather treating
them on general grounds as alternative possible theories.

(a) The view that religion consists in ritual alone
does not result from a study of the more highly
developed religions.   In these ritual may be very important and have a prominent place ; but no one,
probably, would maintain that they ever make ritual
their sole content to the exclusion of creed.   The
theory springs rather from an examination of the
religions of the lower culture : the evidence for it is
" anthropological " in the common sense of that word.
Anthropologists sometimes lay down the principle that
the beliefs of primitive peoples are less worth studying
than their practices.   All ceremonial, whether of primitive or advanced religion, is definite and instructive ;
but to question a savage as to his creed is at best a
waste of time, since his powers alike of self-analysis
and of self-expression are rudimentary, and at worst,
for the same reasons, positively misleading.   How
valuable this principle is every one must recognise who
has compared its practical results with those of the old-

fashioned catechising method.   But in order to explain
its value, anthropologists have sometimes been led to
assert that religion primarily consists in ritual alone,
and that dogma or creed is at first non-existent, and
only arises later through the invention of " ætiological
myth."   The important thing, we are told, is that a
savage does such and such actions at such and such
times ; the story he tells, when pressed by an inquiring
neophyte or a privileged stranger to explain why he
does them, is a subsequent accretion and no part of
the real religious impulse.   Now this explanatory story
or ætiological myth is supposed to be the germ which
develops into creed ; and therefore it follows that creed,
with all its theological and philosophical developments,
is not an integral part of any religion at all.

Such a position, however plausible it may seem at
first sight, involves a host of difficulties.   To begin
with, it is at least unsafe to assume that religion in us
is essentially the same as religion in the savage.   No
proof of this is forthcoming.   It may well be the case
that the emphasis we lay on creed has quite transformed
religion, so that it is to us a different thing, incapable
of explanation by analogy with that of the savage.
Thus anthropologists tell us that the purpose of cloth-
ing, in the most primitive culture, is to attract the eye,
evil or otherwise, of the spectator ; not to keep out
the weather.   Am I therefore to resist the inclination
to wear a greatcoat when I go to the post on a wet
night, on the ground that it is a mere freak of vanity,
and useless because no one will see me ?

Even if the account of savage religion is true, it
does not follow that it is a true account of the religion
of other cultures.   It is useless to appeal to the principle,
if principle it is, that to understand a thing we must
know its history and origin ; for if religion has really
undergone a radical change, that principle is a mere
cloak for giving irrelevant information : the history
offered is the history of something else.

Secondly, such an account of savage religion itself seems to be incomplete. It fails to give any reason why the savage practises his ritual, for *ex hypothesi* the ætiological myth only gives a fictitious reason. No doubt it is possible to say that there is no reason at all, that he has no motive, no special feelings, impelling him to these ceremonies. And it may be true that the accounts given by savages of their motive in ritual are unsatisfactory and inconsistent. But ritual is not mere motiveless play. If it is ritual at all, some definite importance is attached to it ; it is felt to have a value and to be obligatory or necessary. What is the nature of this importance which the savage attaches to his ritual? It cannot be a mere " feeling of importance " in the abstract ; such a feeling is not a possibility. However difficult it may be to explain *why* we feel something to be important, there must be an expressible reason for our feeling ; for instance, the belief that this ritual averts evil consequences of actions done, or ensures benefits of some kind. It is not necessary that the conception be very sharply defined ; but some such conception necessarily underlies every ritual action, and indeed every other action that is not regarded as an end in itself. Ritual is not in this sense an end in itself ; it is not performed as a pleasure but as a necessity ; often as practised by savages a most painful and expensive necessity.

If we could get at the savage's real mind, he would surely reply, when we asked him why he performed certain ceremonies, that otherwise crops would fail, rain would not fall, the spirits which surrround his path and his bed would turn against him. These fears constitute, or rather imply and express, the savage's creed. They, and not ætiological myth, are the germ which develops into creed as we know it. They differ from ætiological myth precisely in this, that whereas they are the real motive of ritual, the latter expresses not the real motive but a fanciful motive, invented when the self-analysis

of the primitive mind has failed to discover the real
one.   That it should try to discover its motive is inevitable ; that it should fail to do so is not surprising.
Nothing is more difficult than to give a reasonable
answer to the question why we behave as we do.   And
the anthropologist is right in refusing to take such
myths as really accounting for ritual ; he is only wrong
if his dissatisfaction with fanciful accounts makes him
doubt the possibility of a true and adequate account.

The point, then, which is independent of any view
as to the relation of magic and religion, because it applies
to both alike, is that ceremonial is based on creed.   It
is not the foundation of creed ; it depends upon it.
The word creed is here used in a quite rudimentary
sense, as indicating any theory of the nature of the
power which governs the universe.   You perform a
ritual act *because* you believe that it pleases that power
and induces it to make rain, or compels it to make rain,
or simply makes rain come automatically ; whatever
particular form your creed takes, it is always creed and
nothing but creed that impels you to ritual.

The principle of the centrality of ritual and the
secondary nature of belief seems thus to be a result of
insufficient analysis ; and though we have examined it
only in its relation to savage religion, it is equally true
of all religion that ritual is explicable by, and founded
in, positive creed ; and that apart from creed ritual
would always be meaningless and unmotived.

(*b*) The second anti-intellectual view of religion
asserts that it is exclusively a matter of conduct, and
that doctrine, so far as it does not immediately bear
upon conduct, is no true part of religion at all.   Now
we may grant at once that religion has much to do with
conduct ; we may even say that no part of it is irrelevant
to conduct ; and yet we may be right in refusing to
expel the intellectual element from it.   For truth and
conduct are not absolutely unrelated.   Every piece of
conduct depends on the realisation of some truth, since

we could not act efficiently, or indeed at all, without
some knowledge of the situation with which we are
dealing.   The problem "How am I to act?" is only
soluble in the light of knowledge.   And conversely
there is no piece of knowledge which has not some
practical corollary ; either it supplies us with the solution of a practical problem, or it suggests a new problem
for future solution.   There is no such thing as conduct
divorced from knowledge or knowledge divorced from
conduct.

The view we are considering seems to depend upon
a form of scepticism.   It admits (and we should agree)
that one action is better than another and that there is
a duty to promote good actions; and it asserts that the
best religion is that which promotes the best life.   But
it goes on to maintain that the doctrines of religion
have no other value except their moral value ; that to
describe one religion as true and another as false is
meaningless.   This implies that the intellectual problems
of religion are insoluble and that no one answer to them
is truer than any other; whereas the practical difficulties
of the moral life are real and can be overcome or
alleviated by religious means.   Or if it is not maintained that the problems are insoluble, it is denied that
religions solve them ; it is perhaps supposed that they
are soluble by means of another kind of thinking; by
science or philosophy.

Empirical difficulties against this purely moral view
of religion arise from the fact that atheists and persons
who differ from their neighbours in religion do not
necessarily differ in morality.   If a man living in a
Christian society rejects Christianity, on this theory
the only possible meaning of his action is that he
rejects the Christian morality, for Christianity is defined
as being precisely the Christian morality.   But in
practice this does not necessarily follow ; his morality
may remain what it was before.   The theory can only
deal with such a case in two ways.   Either it must say

that he rejects Christianity in name only, while unwilling to uproot it out of his heart ; or else it must maintain that he rejects not the real Christianity (the morality) but Christianity falsely so called, the intellectual system which is arbitrarily annexed to it. Both these are unsatisfactory ; the first, because it makes a virtuous atheist into a mere hypocrite, and the second because the "arbitrary" connexion of an intellectual system with a moral one is precisely the fact that requires explanation.

If the intellectual system (though false) is really necessary as a psychological basis for morals,[1] how can the former be rejected and the latter kept ? If not, why should the two ever be united at all ? The moralistic theory of religion comes to grief over the fact that there is such a thing as creed. On the theory, there ought not to be ; but, nevertheless, it is there. Why is it there ? Because—we cannot evade the answer—it is believed to be true. Creed may be, among other things, a means to morality ; but it cannot be a means to anything unless it is first held as true. For a belief that no one believes can have no influence on any one's conduct. A morality assisted by creed is a morality founded upon the intellect ; for to judge something as true is the characteristic function of the intellect.

Further, if the action induced by a belief is to be really good as well as really due to the belief, then the belief must be true. We may stimulate our moral consciousness by fictions, as that this day is our last on earth ; but the resulting action, so far as it is good, is due not to the belief but to the reawakened moral consciousness. Any action really due to the belief, such as taking farewell of our families and making arrange-

---

[1] "It is necessary to most people, but not to every one" is a useless answer, not only because it implies that different people's minds may be constructed on absolutely and radically divergent lines—an assumption which any one is at liberty to make if he likes, and if he will take the trouble to see where it leads him—but because it begs the question. Necessary for some people but not for others, as regular exercise, or a nap after lunch, or a thousand a year, means, as we are using terms, not necessary.

ments for the funeral next day, would be merely silly. So, if our creeds are not truths but only means to good action, those actions which are good are not really due to them, and those which are due to them are a waste of labour. That is to say, they are a hindrance, rather than a help, to right conduct.

This form of scepticism, like most other forms of the same thing, is in fact less a philosophy than a propaganda. It is not a theory of what religion is; it is a proposal to reconstitute it on the principle of leaving out the creed and only keeping the commandments. There might, perhaps, be such a thing as non-religious moral teaching. We will not at present deny that. But it would not be religion. And we are not asking what improvements might be made in religion, or what better thing might be substituted for it; we only want to discover what it is. This humbler inquiry may possibly be of value even to those who, without asking what it is, have decided to abolish or reform it.

(c) The recognition of religion as having an intellectual content throws it open to intellectual criticism; and in order to withdraw it from such criticism it has sometimes been placed in that faculty of the mind whose function is feeling.

The term feeling seems to be distinctively applied by psychologists to pleasure, pain and emotions in general. But emotion is not a totally separate function of the mind, independent of thinking and willing; it includes both these at once. If I feel pleasure, that is will in that it involves an appetition towards the pleasant thing; and it is also knowledge of the pleasant thing and of my own state. There is no emotion which does not entail the activity of the other so-called faculties of the mind. Religion is doubtless an emotion, or rather involves emotions; but it is not emotion in the abstract apart from other activities. It involves, for instance, the love of God. But the love of God implies knowing God on the one hand and doing his will on the other.

Moreover the term itself is ambiguous. The word feeling as we use it in ordinary speech generally denotes not a particular kind of activity, but any state of mind of a somewhat vague, indefinite or indistinct character. Thus we have a feeling of the truth of something when we hardly say yet that we are convinced of its truth ; a feeling of the right treatment of a recalcitrant picture or sonnet, when we are not quite convinced of the right treatment ; a feeling that we ought to do something when we are not really sure. In this sense religion is decidedly not a matter of feeling. Some people's religion is doubtless very nebulous ; but religion as a whole is not distinguished from other things by its vagueness and indefiniteness. Religion is sometimes said to be a "low" degree of thought in the sense that it contains half-truths only, which are in time super-seded by the complete truths of philosophy or science ; but in the meantime it errs (if the description is true) not by being vague but by being much more definite than it has any right to be. To define religion as mere feeling in this sense would amount to complaining that it is not sufficiently dogmatic.

In another commonly-used sense of the word, feeling implies absolute and positive conviction coupled with inability to offer proof or explanation of the conviction. In that case, to "feel" the truth of a statement would merely mean the same as to know it ; and this use of the word therefore already asserts the intellectual content of religion. The problem of the relation of this conviction to proof is noticed below (Part II. Ch. I.).

2. These types of theory all seem to fail through the same fault ; namely, their common denial of the necessity of creed in religion. They describe character-istics which religion does undoubtedly often or always possess ; but they try to explain it as consisting chiefly or only of these characteristics, and to avoid admitting

its basis in positive creed. Without examining further theories of the same kind, therefore, we may venture to assert that religion cannot exist without a definite belief as to the nature of God. This contention would probably be borne out by any careful investigation of actual religions ; every religion claims to present as true and intellectually sound a doctrine which may be described as a theory of God.

This statement of belief as to the nature of God, which of course includes beliefs as to the relations of God and the world, God and man, and so forth, is the intellectual content of religion ; and it is not a thing outside or different from the religion itself. It may be only one aspect or element of religion ; but at least it is an element, and an indispensable element. I call it intellectual, even if it has not been reached by " scientific " processes, because the intellect is the name of that activity by which we think, know, hold convictions or draw inferences ; and a non-intellectual conviction would be a contradiction in terms.[1]

Now the Doctrine of God is of course theology ; it is in fact the translation of that word. Accordingly, a creed is a theology, and there is no distinction whatever between Theology and Religion, so far as the intellectual aspect of religion is concerned. My theology is the beliefs I hold about God, that is to say, my creed, the intellectual element of my religion.

This identification is often controverted. In the first place, a distinction is sometimes made between religion and theology with a view to reconciling the claims of criticism with those of ecclesiastical authority. Criticism (it is supposed) merely affects theology ; orthodoxy is a matter of religion and is untouched by critical arguments. Such a distinction enables us to make two promises : first, to believe whatever the

---

[1] The word intellect is sometimes used to distinguish one type of cognition from other types called reason, intuition and so on. Such distinctions are, in my belief, based on mistaken psychology ; and accordingly I use the various words indiscriminately to cover the whole of the facts of knowing.

church believes ; and secondly, to accept whatever criticism proves. But the two spheres cannot be separated in this way. There is an abstract possibility that criticism should prove the Gospel a forgery and that philosophy should demonstrate God to be an illusion ; and the second promise involves readiness to accept these results as promptly as any others. But this implication already denies any weight to the authority of the church ; for no church would allow its members to accept such conclusions. The proposed *modus vivendi* is as valueless in practice as it is indefensible in theory.

Some writers, again, distinguish theology, as the thought which takes religion as its starting-point and builds a superstructure upon it, from the religion upon which it builds. But this is no distinction at all ; for if religion supplies the premisses from which theology infers other new truths, the two are only related as premisses and conclusion in one syllogism, and one and the same syllogism cannot be split up into two distinct kinds of thought. Rather, this argument would prove the identity of the two ; for there is no difference between putting together the premisses and drawing the conclusion. It is only in the abstractions of formal logic that they are separated. The distinction therefore would be an entirely abstract one; we could never point to two different concrete things and say "this is religion and that theology."

The same objection would apply to the opposite distinction, according to which theology, instead of using religion as its starting-point, takes its pronouncements as conclusions, and endeavours to provide proofs for them. This does seem to be a way in which the word theology is sometimes used ; thus the conviction of the existence of God might be described as religion, and the proofs of his existence as theology. But in that case theology would include the whole intellectual side of religion in itself, and religion would be merely the name for an incomplete and mutilated fragment of theology—the conclusion without the evidence—which when its deficiencies were made good would coincide with theology.

A somewhat similar distinction is that between religion as the personal experience of the individual and theology as the systematic statement of religious experience as a whole. If religion means "that fragment of theology, of whose truth I have had personal experience," the distinction between the two can never be made at all. Theology is the whole; religion my particular part of it. *For me*—within my knowledge—the two are in every way identical. Whatever theology I know is to me religion; and the rest I do not know.

There is certainly a kind of thought which takes religious dogmas and tries to discover their logical result; and one which tries to prove their truth; and one which arranges and expresses them all in a systematic way. And if we like to call any or all of these theology, we have no doubt a right to do so. But we must remember, if we use the term, that theology so described is not different from religion. A religious truth does not cease to be religious truth and turn into theological truth because it is proved, or arranged in a system, or reflected upon.

In general, then, it does not seem that we can distinguish religion as creed from theology at all. Each of the above distinctions, as we have said, does correspond to a real difference in the way in which we use the words; and they may be summed up by saying that in ordinary language religion means something less deliberate, less consciously logical, than theology. Religious experience gives us a number of truths arranged anyhow, just as they come to the surface; all is knowledge, all the fruit of intellectual activity, since intellect means nothing but the attainment of knowledge; but it is knowledge unsystematised. Theology then, according to this view, arranges and

classifies the truths already given in religion ; it creates
nothing new, but rather, so to speak, tidies up the
workshop where religion has finished work for the
day. But even this simile overstates the difference;
for in the apparent chaos of the unsystematised
experience, system is in fact already present. The
work of co-ordination which we have ascribed to
theology is already characteristic of religion itself; it
supplies us not with a number of disconnected conceptions of the nature of God, but with *a* conception.

3. (*a*) If religion as creed is identical with theology,
it remains to consider the further conception of the
philosophy of religion. The philosophy of any subject
means careful reflexion upon that subject ; thus we
have the philosophy of art, of conduct, of science and
so on. To do a thing, and to understand what one
is doing and how one does it, seem to be different
things ; and this distinction, it is thought, can be
applied to intellectual as well as practical processes.
To commit a crime is action ; to reflect upon one's
crime is ethics. Similarly, to conduct an argument is
science, to reflect upon it is logic ; to be conscious of
God is religion, to analyse that consciousness is the
philosophy of religion. Such is the common doctrine ;
but it does not seem to provide us with a basis for
distinguishing the philosophy of religion from other
philosophies. Consciousness of truths is common to
religion and all other kinds of thought ; the only
distinction between religious and other knowledge
would be that they were concerned with different
objects. But the theory of knowledge or logic does
not consider differences of the object, but only processes of the subject ; and therefore there is no distinction between the philosophy of religion (as theory
of religious knowledge) and the theory of knowledge
in general. If there is a general philosophy of knowing, it includes religious knowledge as well as all
other kinds ; no separate philosophy is required.

Similarly, if religion involves certain types of conduct, the whole theory of conduct in general is treated by ethics. That side of the philosophy of religion merges in ethics precisely as the intellectual side merges in the general theory of knowledge or logic. There can only be a distinct philosophy of religion if religion is a quite separate function of the mind involving neither knowledge, volition, or any other specifiable activity. But unless this hypothesis can be maintained (and we know already that it cannot), we must give up the idea of a special departmental philosophy, the philosophy of religion, and hand over the study of religion to philosophy in general.

(*b*) If the philosophy of religion is indistinguishable from philosophy as a whole, what is the relation of philosophy as a whole to religion or theology? Philosophy is the theory of existence ; not of existence in the abstract, but of existence in the concrete ; the theory of all that exists ; the theory of the universe. This is frequently denied ; it is said that philosophy has problems of its own, and science has problems of its own ; that they progress by attending each to its own business and using its methods where they are suitable, and that when philosophy tries to answer the questions proper to science the result is chaos. The example of natural science under the domination of Aristotelian philosophy in the later middle ages is quoted as a warning to philosophy to confine its activities within its own province.—Such a view seems to depend on a misconception as to the nature of philosophy. Sciences live by the discovery and employment of methods which facilitate their particular operations and are inapplicable to other kinds of research. Differentiation of problems and methods is the very essence of the natural sciences. It is important to realise that philosophy has in this sense no methods of its own at all ; that it is through and through homogeneous, straightforward thinking where formulæ and labour-saving devices are not used. This absence of definite and ready-made method is at once the strength and the weakness of philosophy ; its weakness, because it makes philosophy much more difficult than any of the sciences ; its strength, because failure through defects in the apparatus is avoided, and there is no limitation to one particular subject such as is necessarily entailed by a fixed method. Philosophy is the free activity of critical thought, and is applicable to any problem which thought can raise. The chaos of which the scientist complains is partly his own feeling of helplessness when confronted by philosophical questions to which his methods supply no answer, and partly real blunders like those of mediæval science, whose cause he imagines to be the invasion of science by Aristotelian philosophy ; whereas they are really due not to the overbearingness of Aristotelian philosophy but to the defects of Aristotelian science.

Now if philosophy is the theory of the universe, what is religion ? We have said that it was the theory[1] of God, and of God's relations to the world and man. But the latter is surely nothing more nor less than a view of the universe. Indeed religion is quite as comprehensive as philosophy. For the religious consciousness in its true and complete form nothing is irrelevant, nothing is without its own unique and individual value. Religion and philosophy alike are views of the whole universe.

But are they therefore (it may be asked) identical ? May they not be views, but conflicting views? or views from different points of view? Not the latter, because it is the aim of each alike to transcend particular points of view, to overcome the limitations of individual interest. And to ask whether religion and

---

[1] It is possibly worth while to guard against a verbal pitfall. "Philosophy is theory, but religion is not ; it is Fact." This common—and wrong—use of the word seems to imply that a theory ceases to be a theory when it is true, or when it is a matter of vital interest or strong conviction. It was Mephistopheles who said, " Grau, theurer Freund, ist alle Theorie, und grün des Lebens goldner Baum."

philosophy may not disagree is to assume a general
agreement among religions, which certainly does not
exist, and the same among philosophies, which exists
if possible even less. No doubt this or that philosophy
would conflict with this or that religion. The religion
of Homer is inconsistent with the philosophy of
Auguste Comte ; but Comte's own religion and his
philosophy are fully consistent with one another ; they
are indeed identical. If religion and philosophy are
views of the same thing—the ultimate nature of the
universe—then the true religion and the true philosophy
must coincide, though they may differ in the vocabulary
which they use to express the same facts.

But, it may be insisted, we have at least by this
enforced agreement condemned unheard all philosophies
but those which believe in a God ; for we have defined
religion as the theory of God, and many philosophies
deny or doubt or never mention God. This difficulty
may perhaps be cleared up by recollecting that we
have not assumed the " existence of God " hitherto in
any definite and concrete sense ; we have not, for
instance, assumed a personal God. The God of whom
we have been speaking was a purely abstract one, a
mere name for the philosophical Absolute, the solution
of the cosmological problem. Thus we said that
savage ritual (religious or magical) implies a creed ;
but it may not imply anything we should call a theistic
creed. The savage may believe that his ritual operates
directly on the rain without any intervention on the
part of a single supreme will. This is his " theory of
God " ; his " God " is not a person but a principle.
The Buddhist believes in no personal God at all, but
he has a definite scheme of the universe and doctrine
of salvation ; he believes in certain eternal principles ;
that is his " theory of God." Atheism itself, if it is a
positive theory and not mere scepticism, is in this
abstract sense a " theory of God " ; the only thing that
is not a theory of God is scepticism, that is to say, the

refusal to deal with the problem at all. God, so far as our conception has travelled, is merely at present a name for the unifying principle of the world, however that principle is regarded. Every philosophy has a God in this sense, just in so far as it is a philosophy and not a mere collocation of disconnected doctrines ; in which case it has a number of different Gods whose relations it has not yet determined. And this is the only sense in which some religions (such as Buddhism) have a God. In the sense, then, in which all religions require a God, one is equally required by all philosophy.

(c) Since religion, on its intellectual side, is a theory of the world as a whole, it is the same thing as philosophy ; the ultimate questions of philosophy are those of religion too. But can we say the same of science ? Is not science, at least as interpreted by many of its exponents, anti-religious in its materialism and its frequent atheism ; and even if these characteristics were not present, does it not differ necessarily from both religion and philosophy in being a view of the universe not as a whole but in minute particular details only ?

To the first question it must be replied that, paradoxical though it may seem, materialism and atheism are not necessarily irreligious. Philosophy, as well as science, may be both materialist and atheist ; indeed there may be, as we have said, religions which show the same features. We may even be so bold as to assert that atheism and materialism are necessarily religions of a kind ; for not only do they spring from the impulse to solve the intellectual problem of the universe, but they owe their form to an essentially religious dissatisfaction with existing solutions. Thus an atheist may well be an atheist because he has a conception of God which he cannot reconcile with the creeds of other people ; because he feels that the ground of the universe is too mysterious, too august to be described in terms of human personality and encumbered with mythological impertinences. The materialist, again, may find in matter a real object of worship, a thing more worthy of admiration than the God of popular religion. The materialist Lucretius adores not the careless gods of the interstellar space, but the "alma Venus," the immanent principle of nature itself. And can we deny that such materialism or atheism is more truly religious, does more honour to the true God, than many theistic superstitions?

The materialism and atheism of modern science—if indeed these qualities are rightly ascribed to it, which is very doubtful—may or may not be preferable, considered as a view of the universe, to that offered by traditional Christianity. But whichever is right, each alike is a religion, and it is only because of this fact that they can ever come into conflict.

In reply to the second question, the suggestion that science, as the knowledge of detail, is irrelevant to philosophy the knowledge of the whole, and therefore not itself religious in character, it must be remembered that we cannot have a whole which is not a whole of parts, nor parts which are not parts of a whole. Philosophy, as well as science, is concerned with detail ; it does not exist in the rarefied atmosphere of a world aloof from facts. Nor does science take its facts in absolute isolation one from another and from a general scheme of the world ; it is essential to science that the facts should be related to one another and should find each its place in the scientist's view of the whole. And any religion must take account of detail ; for it is only in the details that the nature of the whole is manifested.

It is no doubt possible to forget the whole in laying stress on isolated parts, as it is possible to forget details in the general view of a whole. But each of these is a false abstraction ; we cannot identify the former with science and the latter with religion or philosophy. The ideal, alike for philosophy and science, is to see the part in its place in the whole, and the whole perfectly exemplified in the part.

CHAPTER II

WE have arrived at the conclusion that all religion has an intellectual element ; that this element is a creed or theology and at the same time a cosmology or philosophical theory of the world ; and that therefore religion is so far identical with philosophy. But we have still to determine what other elements it contains, and how these elements are related to one another.

Religion, we are told again and again, is more than mere intellect, more than mere thought, more than philosophy. It may indeed find room within itself for an intellectual element, but that is not the whole of religion ; there are other elements of equal value. Indeed, intellect is only one single aspect of life ; and if philosophers sometimes treat it as if nothing else existed, that is only because philosophers are human enough to magnify their office. Granting freely that religion has its intellectual side, it has also a practical side which is no less important.

If this language is justified, religion is not merely a theory of the world ; it is also a system of conduct. Just as any definite religion prescribes to its adherents certain definite convictions, so it inculcates certain definite modes of action. We have to ask whether this is true ; and if we find that religion does really contain these two distinct elements, we shall be compelled to determine so far as possible the nature of their connexion.

1. Parallel to the anti-intellectual theories examined in the preceding chapter are certain anti-moral theories of religion. These are directed to proving that religion does not dictate definite actions at all, or that if it does, this is not because these actions are moral but for some other reason.

(*a*) As a matter of common experience, it is often said, religion sometimes inculcates actions which are flagrantly at variance with the principles of a sound morality. Can we look back on all the crimes done in the name of religion, the human sacrifices, the persecutions, the horrors of religious warfare, the corrupt connivance at wickedness, the torture inflicted on simple minds by the fear of hell—*tantum relligio potuit suadere malorum*—and still maintain that religion stands for morality? Undoubtedly we can. The argument is a rhetorical jump from half-understood instances to an unfounded generalisation. We might equally well quote the absurdities of ancient and the errors of modern scientists as proof that science does not aim at truth. If a great scientist makes a mistake, the importance of that mistake, its widespread effect, is due to the very fact that the man who makes it is a high intellectual authority ; it is the exception which proves the rule that you can generally believe what he says. Religious persecution may be a crime, but it happens only because the persecutor believes it to be a duty. The crimes of the Church are a testimony to the fact that religion does dictate duties, and is believed to do so, for the most part, in a worthy manner.

Nor can we draw a distinction between the two cases on the ground that religious crimes are sometimes already condemned by their contemporaries and are therefore doubly unjustifiable, whereas the mistakes of a great scientist represent a point in the progress of thought as yet unattained by any one, and are therefore pardonable. This would be to reduce the argument to a mutual recrimination between Church and State, each trying to fasten upon the other the odium of being the worse sinner. Into such a discussion we can hardly be expected to enter. Our distinction is between right and wrong, truth and falsehood; and if science teaches error or religion inculcates crime, extenuating circumstances are beside the mark.

If the argument were successful, it would prove not that religion was irrelevant to conduct (for the cases quoted prove the reverse; they are cases of religion definitely dictating conduct), but that it devoted its energies to the positive pursuit of immoral ends. And this would be to admit our main contention, that religion has a practical side; while maintaining that this practical side was the apotheosis not of good but of evil. But this fantastic notion would be advanced by no serious student of the facts, and we need not trouble to refute it. We are not concerned to prove that every particular mouthpiece of every particular religion is morally infallible; just as we do not assume it to be intellectually infallible. We tried to show in the last chapter that it was an essential note of religion to lay down certain statements, and to say, " Believe these "; and that could only mean, " Believe these, for they are true." Truth is the governing conception, even if the dogmas propounded fail of reaching it. Similarly, religion always lays down certain courses of action and says, " Do these," that is to say, " Do these, because they are right." Not *merely* " because they are God's will," for God is a righteous God; nor *merely* " for fear he should punish you," for his punishments are just.

Historically, religions may have been guilty of infinite crimes; but this condemnation is a proof, not a disproof, that their fundamental aim is moral. They represent a continual attempt to conform to the good will of God, and the fact that they err in determining or in obeying that will does not alter the fact that the standard by which they test actions is a moral standard. But is the will of God always conceived as good? May it not be conceived as simply arbitrary? One phase of this question is considered in the next section.

(*b*) A second argument, of a type somewhat akin to the last, is drawn from anthropology. It appears that in primitive societies the morality of the tribe develops on lines independent of its religion. It is therefore supposed that morality and religion are two quite different things, which only in course of time come to be united in what is called the "moralisation of religion." This argument takes it for granted—and indeed it can hardly be questioned—that the higher religions *are* moralised; that they conceive God's will as necessarily good.

As in the last chapter, we may dismiss this argument by showing that it is irrelevant. For us religion is already moralised, and we must accept it as it is and not pretend that religion as known to us is still the same thing that (on the theory) it is to the savage.

But as in the case of the anti-intellectual argument from anthropology we were not content with dismissing it as irrelevant, but found it necessary to inquire more carefully into its own statements, so here it is desirable not simply to dismiss but to examine the argument. The word "moralisation" is the real difficulty. If a thing has at the outset nothing to do with morality, no jugglery or alchemy will bring it into relation with the moral consciousness. You cannot arbitrarily impose a category on a thing which is unfitted to receive it. And to suggest that "social evolution" can confer a moral value on a type of activity which has as yet no moral bearings whatever, is calling in a *deus ex machina* to perform feats which involve a contradiction in terms.

The moralisation of religion—the bringing of it into conformity with our moral standards—is certainly a real thing. But it is not a single event, once for all accomplished, in which religion leaves behind its old indifference to morality and learns to take cognisance of moral values. It is a continual process in which old standards are left behind and better ones adopted. If we look at the conduct of a class or nation or culture very different from our own, we are apt to imagine for a moment that it has no morality at all. But what we mistake for an absence of morality is really the presence of a different morality. Primitive religion does not inculcate civilised morality ; why should it ? It inculcates primitive morality ; and as the one grows the other grows too.

(c) We now pass to a group of theories which arise not from the external, historical or psychological, investigation of the religious consciousness, but within that consciousness itself. These are determinist, antinomian, and quietist respectively.

Religious determinism results from a conviction of the omnipotence and universality of God, so interpreted that no power of initiation whatever is left to the human will. All that is done is done by God ; God's plans are not conditional upon man's co-operation or overthrown by his rebellion, because God knew these things before, and indeed was himself the cause of them. This creed lays upon its adherent no commands in the ordinary sense of the word, for it does not hold him free to execute them. On the other hand, it does issue commands in the only sense in which it allows itself to do so ; it teaches that one type of conduct is pleasing to God and another unpleasing, so that, if a man were free to choose, it would not hesitate to point out the kind of behaviour that ought to be chosen. And indeed those who hold views of this kind often surpass all others in the rigorism and puritanism of their actual lives. This theory therefore does not really banish conduct from religion.

(d) Antinomianism springs from the same conception, as to the relation between God's will and man's, which underlies determinism. It causes, therefore, no fresh difficulty. But it is perhaps desirable to point out the element of truth which it contains. If morality is conceived as what St. Paul calls a "law of works," an external and apparently unreasonable code of imperatives, then such a morality is certainly, as the antinomian believes, superseded and done away by religion. The external, compulsive law has been replaced by an inner spring of life. If a man is perfectly religious it is true that it does not matter what he does; not in the sense that he may commit crimes with impunity, but in the sense that he will not commit them, even if you forget to tell him not to. Thus religion appears as a release from the servitude of morality.

But this view depends on a false description of morality. The man to whose mind a moral law is a mere external command, grudgingly obeyed under compulsion, falls short not merely of religion but of morality. He is not really moral at all. He is in a state of heteronomy; it is not his own will, freely acting, that produces the result but the imposition upon his will of alien force. The very nature of the moral law is this, that it is not imposed upon us from without. We do not merely obey it; we make it. The member of the "kingdom of ends," the truly moral society, is not a mere subject; he is a sovereign. Thus the moral law has already that character of spontaneity, that absence of compulsion, which is typical of religion. The transition from heteronomy to autonomy which for St. Paul is marked by the passage from Judaism to Christianity—from the law of works to the law of faith—is not a transition from morality to religion, but a transition into morality from some infra-moral state.

What, then, is this infra-moral state? We might be tempted to describe it as the stage of positive law, of civil law. But this would be equally unsatisfactory. Just as the really moral consciousness makes its own laws, and does not merely obey them blindly, so the really social will finds in the law of its society its own self-expression, and is sovereign as well as subject in the state in which it lives.   This is an ideal, doubtless, to which few societies attain ; but it is the ideal, none the less, of civil life as such.   And, therefore, we cannot distinguish civil from moral law as characterised by heteronomy and autonomy respectively.

The difference is not between two types of law but between differences of attitude to one and the same law. The law may be divine, moral, or civil ; in each case there are two ways of obeying it, either from within, when the law becomes the free self-expression of the acting will, or from without, the law appearing as a tyrannical force blindly and grudgingly obeyed.   This is the distinction which the antinomian has in mind.

Antinomianism in the commonest sense, however, makes the mistake of supposing that the transition to autonomy cancels the duties which heteronomy enforced. Even this is in one sense true, for any " law of works " contains numbers of superfluous commands, presenting as duties actions which the autonomous will rightly sees to be valueless.   But in so far as the external law enjoins real duties, the internal law comes not to destroy but to fulfil.   Thus whatever in morality is really moral is taken up into religion ; and the state of mind which marks it as religious, the free and joyful acceptance of it, is not peculiar to religion as distinct from morality.   It is essential to morality as such.

(e) It remains to examine the view known as quietism.   This view may be analysed as a development from certain types of expression very common in all religion ; for instance, that religion is not self-assertion but self-surrender ; that in the religious life we wait upon God and accept his good will instead of imposing ours upon him ; that the individual is lost in union with God, and is no longer an independent will.   Such language is often called mysticism, and the word may be usefully employed in this sense. It is, however, well to remember that the experience to which this language refers is an experience not peculiar to certain people called mystics, but common to every religious mind. Subject to this caution, we may use the word mystical as a description of that aspect of the religious life which consists in the fusion of the individual with God.

This question is one which we shall treat at length in a later chapter ; and we shall there see reason to believe that this mystical language, so far from being a fanciful or confused description of the facts, gives a perfectly accurate account of that relation to God which is the essence of personal religion. At present we are concerned not with mysticism but with its offshoot, or rather perversion, quietism. Mysticism asserts the union of my will with the will of God, the total and complete fusion of the two into one. Quietism asserts that my will is negated, that it has simply disappeared and the will of God has taken its place. I am utterly lost in the infinity of God. The two things are really quite distinct ; the former asserts a union of two wills in one person, the latter asserts that the person has only one will, and that not his own but God's. Theologians will recall the relation of the Monothelite heresy[1] to the orthodox Christology of the Church; and indeed we may suggest that quietism was only a revival in another context of the essential doctrine of Monothelitism, whereas mysticism exactly expresses the orthodox view as to the relation of the divine and human wills.

Quietism thus denies that conduct is a part of religion, because it believes that in religion the individual will disappears; religion is a state of complete passivity. This doctrine is due to the assumption (which we shall criticise later) that two wills cannot be fused into one,

---

[1] Consisting in the assertion that Christ had not (as laid down at Chalcedon) two wills, one human and one divine, but one only, the divine, and no human will at all. This was heretical as destroying the humanity of Christ. The subject is treated below in Part III. Ch. I.

and therefore, feeling bound to preserve the unity of
the individual, the quietist denies the human and keeps
the divine.   Pending our inquiry into the underlying
principle, it is enough to point out certain objections.
(i.) The act of self-abnegation is definitely an act of
will, and is represented as a duty, and a religious duty ;
therefore the practical content of religion is not in
point of fact denied.   (ii.) This act is not done once
for all ; it is a continual attitude of the self to God,
an attitude capable of being discontinued by an act of
will, and therefore itself maintained by an act of will.
(iii.) The union with God thus attained does not
deprive the individual of all activity.   Rather it directs
and makes more fruitful and potent this activity.   It
affords a solution of all his practical difficulties, and
gives him the strength to carry out the solution ; but
it does not remove them from his consciousness and
place him in a simply inactive sphere of life.   In a
word, the self-dedication of the will to God is not the
end of the individual life, but the beginning of a new
and indeed of a more active life.   The union with God
is a real union, not the annihilation of the self.

2. We have perhaps sufficiently shown that religion
never exists apart from conduct.   Just as all religion
involves thought, as every religion teaches doctrine and
a true religion teaches true doctrine, so all religion involves conduct ; and whereas a good religion teaches
good conduct, a bad religion teaches bad.   And further,
just as we found that all knowledge was already in
essence religious, so we must now say that all morality
is already religious ; for, as we have seen, morality
properly understood already shows in itself the freedom,
the autonomy and devotion, of religion.   It seems, therefore, that religion is not a simple but a complex thing,
containing two (or, for all we yet know, more) different
elements.   It is necessary that we should do something
towards determining the relation of these elements to
one another.   If they are really separate ingredients of

a compound, then religion is merely the name for a life which contains both thought and action side by side ; it is no third thing over and above these, but simply the one *plus* the other.   Such a conclusion really negates the conception of religion altogether ; for the different independent elements of which it is composed are capable of complete analysis and description each by itself, and there is no whole (religion) but only parts (thought, action).

As a means of approach to this difficulty, it would be well to ask whether it is necessary that the two elements should always coexist ; or whether they are alternative modes of operation which can only exist one at a time, so that to speak of a kind of consciousness which unites the two, as we maintain that religion does, is meaningless.

(*a*) In any case of action, it is easy to see that some thought must be present.   When we discussed the ritualistic theory of religion we found that unless ritual was simply meaningless and unmotived play it must be based on some definite creed.   We may extend this principle further.   Unless action is based on some knowledge it cannot take place at all.   The most that can happen is some automatism of which the person, whose action we call it, is unconscious.   An action is necessarily based on a large number of judgments, of which some must be true or the action could not be carried out ; while others may be true or false but must at least be believed.   If, for instance, a man wants to drown himself, he must know " here lies the water : good : here stands the man : good " : otherwise he is not able to do it ; and also he must believe rightly or wrongly that he will improve his circumstances and get rid of his present miseries by putting an end to his life ; otherwise he will not desire to do it.   Thus every act depends for its conception and execution upon thought.   It is not merely that first we think and then we act ; the thinking goes on all through the act.   And therefore, in general, the conception of any activity as practical alone, and containing no elements of knowing or thinking, is indefensible.   Our actions depend on our knowledge.

(*b*) The converse is equally true.   If we can only do what we know how to do, we only know what we wish to know.   Knowing is an activity just as walking is, and, like walking, requires to be set in motion by the operation of the will.   To think requires effort; it can be described as harder or easier ; it is the outcome of a choice which deliberately determines to think and selects a subject of thought.   There can be no activity of thought apart from activity of the will.

If this is so, it is no longer possible to uphold the familiar distinction between a life of thought and a life of action.   The man of action, the statesman or the soldier, would never be able to act at all but for his intellectual grip on the problems of his profession.   The best man of action is not simply the man of iron will, dear to the popular imagination, but the man who has the clearest insight into the necessities and peculiarities of the given situation.   Indeed the notion of a strong will in itself, apart from strength of intellect, and still more the worship of an abstract " will to power " or " blind will," are mere absurdities.   A will to power must know what kinds of power there are to have, and which kind it wants ; and a blind will that did not know what it was doing or what there was to be done would never do anything at all.   The student or man of contemplation, on the other hand, does not simply know without willing.   He wills to know ; and his knowledge is the result of positive hard labour.   No moment of thought is conceivable which is not also a volition, and no moment of will is possible which is not also an act of knowledge.

Thus if there is such a thing as the religious life, it must be one which, like any other, involves both thinking and acting ; and the religious life, so conceived, is

not, any more than a philosopher's life or a statesman's, the mere sum of two different lives. For of
the two ingredients neither can ever exist by itself. It
must exist in union with the other or not at all. Any
real life must contain both elements, each playing as
important a part as the other.

3. But although the duality, of which religion now
seems to consist, cannot be broken up, in the concrete,
into two separable elements, it is still a duality.
Thought and action remain simply side by side and
absolutely distinct, though each is necessary to the
other. Religion, it appears, is simply a compound of
philosophy and morality, though philosophy always involves morality and morality can never exist without
philosophy ; and therefore all life, as such, shows the
composite character which is the mark of religion. It
is not simply religion, but all the life of the mind, that
is now subject to the dualism ; and therefore there is
the greater need of understanding it. What is this
dualism between thought and action ? We have seen
that the two things mutually depend upon one another,
but we have not inquired very minutely into the nature
of this dependence.

(a) In the theory of the religious life offered by
religion itself, there is no dualism at all between knowing and acting. The two things are united, for instance
by the author of the fourth Gospel, in such a way that
they are absolutely indistinguishable. The term used
to express their unity is "love," an activity which in
its perfect manifestation is represented as the perfection
of the religious life. The whole of the great final
discourse in John is an exposition of this conception ;
nothing can be clearer than the way in which the spirit
of love is identified on the one hand with that of truth,
and on the other with that of morality or obedience.
And the two elements are not connected merely externally ; knowledge is the way of obedience and
obedience the approach to truth. The connexion

between the two is the most intimate conceivable ; just as the perfect life involves the denial of all distinction between man 'and man, so it involves the denial of all distinction between man's two faculties of thought and will.

(*b*) Such denials of our ordinary distinction, even if they cannot in themselves be taken as conclusive, serve at least to arouse doubts as to its sufficiency. And if we ask how thought and action are actually distinguished, the answer is not very satisfying. They are not the operations of two different parts of the mind ; that is admitted on all hands. The whole self wills, and the whole self thinks. Then are they alternative activities, like sleeping and waking ? No ; we have already seen that they are necessarily and always simultaneous. The only thing we can say seems to be that thinking is not willing and willing is not thinking. And this is simply to assert the existence of a distinction without explaining wherein the distinction consists. We cannot say that in willing we do not think, or that in thinking we do not will, for both these, as we have seen, we certainly do.

If I will to think, there are not two elements in this act but one. When I will to walk, I do not separately experience an internal resolve on the one hand, and a movement of my legs on the other ; the act of will *is* the voluntary moving of the legs. To say "I will to walk" is the same thing as saying "I walk of my own initiative," that is, "I walk." And so "I will to think" means not two things but one thing : "I think." We never simply will in the abstract ; we always will to do something ; what we turn into a separate organ and call "the will" is only the fact of free activity, the voluntary doing of this thing or that. Walking is thus not something distinguishable from willing, a result, so to speak, of the operation of "the will" ; it is nothing more nor less than the willing itself, the particular form which, on this occasion, free activity

D

takes. Thus walking is a kind of willing, not something else ; and equally, thought is a kind of willing.

But is there any other kind of willing ? Walking
is only one kind ; is thinking only one kind? No ;
for if it were, there would be kinds of willing in which
thought was not present. This, we have already
admitted, there cannot be; and therefore, just as all
thinking is willing, so all willing is thinking. Or, to
put it in other words, there is neither consciousness
nor activity considered as a separate reality, but always
the activity of consciousness and the consciousness of
activity. Nor can we say that in this second case there
is a dualism between the activity of a mind and its own
consciousness of that activity ; for an activity is already
by its very nature conscious of itself, and if it were
not, it would be not an activity but a mechanism.

We conclude, therefore, not that one and the same
thing, mind, has two manifestations, consciousness and
volition, and that these two always exist side by side,
but that all consciousness is volitional, and that all
volition is conscious. The distinction between the two
statements is not merely verbal. The former way of
putting it suggests that there is such a thing as a mind,
regarded as a thing in itself ; and that this thing has
two ways of behaving, which go on at once, as a
machine might have both a circular and a reciprocating
motion. This idea of the mind as a thing distinguishable from its own activities does not seem to be really
tenable ; the mind *is* what it *does* ; it is not a thing
that thinks, but a consciousness ; not a thing that wills,
but an activity.

(*c*) This somewhat tedious discussion was necessary
in order to vindicate the real unity of the religious life
against the view that it is a falsely conceived juxtaposition of heterogeneous functions with no unity and
no interconnexion. There is, we have argued, only
one kind of activity ; namely, that which is at the same
time thought and will, knowledge and action; and if

religion is the name of this activity, then all true life is religion. We cannot distinguish three kinds of life, the thinking life, the active life, and the religious life that unites the two. So far as anybody thinks, he wills to think, and is so far already in possession of the complete or religious life; and the same is true of any one who wills.

It may be desirable to remark at this point that to say there is only one possible complete life, and that the religious, does not in the least abolish the differences between different people's abilities and ideals, or set up one out of a number of lives as the one to which all ought to conform. In a sense, it is to do the very opposite of this; for we have pointed out that whatever life is really livable, whatever is a life at all, is already for that very reason religious in its degree; and that no one type of life has any right to claim for itself the title of religious at the expense of any other.

In one sense we do certainly make a restriction in the variety of ideals; not in the number of possible lives, but in the ways in which such lives may be classified. While fully agreeing that there is a difference between the work of a statesman and that of a philosopher, for instance, we should not admit that this difference is of such a kind that the former can be correctly described as a man of action and the latter as a man of thought. And in the same way, we should not wish to deny the difference between a priest and a layman; but we should deny that the life of the one was religious and the life of the other secular. As every life includes, and indeed is, both thought and action, so every life is essentially religious; and the secular life, if that means a life negatively defined by the mere absence of religion, does not exist at all. If, however, the "secular" life is defined positively as consisting of interests from which priests are excluded, or of interests lying altogether outside the sphere of religion, we shall reply that no legitimate interest is foreign to all religious life ; and that the question what is and what is not lawful for a priest, though a perfectly legitimate question, cannot be decided by an appeal to the conception of religion. Every man has his own duties, and every class of men has duties proper to itself as a class ; but just as the "man of action" is not freed from the obligation to truth, nor the "man of contemplation" from the obligation to morality, so the layman is as much bound as the priest by the ideals of the religion which in some form or other he cannot help professing.

CHAPTER III

We have till now, in our treatment of the intellectual side of religion, confined our attention to the philosophic or theological content ; but if we are right in supposing the religious life to be all-inclusive, it must also include the activity of historical thought. Religion, as Coleridge says, must contain " facts " as well as " ideas."

The historical aspect of religion is not likely to suffer neglect at the present time. The application to religious problems of historical research has been the most conspicuous and brilliant feature in the theology of the last half-century. Even thirty years ago, so little was generally known of the origins and antecedents of Christianity that when the Apocalypse of Enoch was first produced in English in 1883, its editor could gloat with an almost comic delight over the publication of " the Semitic romance from which Jesus of Nazareth borrowed his conceptions of the triumphant return of the Son of Man." To-day no writer, however ignorant of recent research, could compose such a sentence. Every one knows that Christianity was deeply rooted in Judaism, and the relations of the two can be discussed without shocking the orthodox or causing malicious glee to the critics.

This great historical movement in theology has taken two chief forms. They cannot indeed be sharply separated, but they may be broadly distinguished for the sake of convenience. One is Comparative Religion,

37

with its anthropological and psychological branches ; the other is Historical Theology, concentrating upon the antecedents, origin, history, and development of Christian doctrine.   Each of these has made enormous and most valuable contributions to theology ; indeed whatever progress has been made in the last fifty years has been due almost entirely to their help.

1. The danger at the present time is not so much that the religious importance of history may be. forgotten as that it may be overrated.   The great successes of historical theology and of comparative religion sometimes lead theologians to expect more from these methods than they ever really supply.   There is a tendency to regard historical methods as the only respectable approach to religious truth ; to suppose that the vexed questions of theology are soluble by historical means or not at all ; in fact to imagine that theology has tried the method of speculation and found it wanting, and that it has now at length found the right method, a method which properly used will yield all the truth that can ever be known.

This theory I shall describe as historical positivism, by analogy with Comte's view that human thought was in his time emerging from a " metaphysical " stage and entering on a " positive " ; casting aside barren *a priori* speculation and waking up at last to the reality and all-sufficiency of *a posteriori* science ; passing out of the region of ideas into the region of facts.   Comte's forecast, it may be observed in passing, was just. Thought did from his time assume for a while a notably less metaphysical and more positive character.   It had been well frightened by its own philosophical daring in the previous period.   It had jumped in and found itself out of its depth ; and Comte was the mouthpiece by which it recorded its vow never to try to swim again.   Who has not made a similar vow ? and who, after making it, has ever kept it ?

As in the case of Comtian positivism, so this

historical positivism in theology seems to imply a definitely anti-philosophical scepticism ; it is a merely negative attitude. It is characteristic of two religious types which at first sight seem to have little in common. On the one hand, it is expressed by that extreme anti-speculative orthodoxy which takes its stand on the bald historical fact "so the Church believes and has believed"; on the other, it is found in the extreme anti-dogmatic view of many Liberal Protestants, to whom "metaphysic" is anathema. These positions we shall not criticise in detail. We have already laid down in a former chapter the necessity to religion of a speculative creed, and there is no need to repeat the arguments there used. Instead of proving the impossibility of a totally un-philosophical theology, we shall consider two instances of unphilosophical representations of religion and try to show where and why they break down. These instances are abstract or one-sided forms of the two sciences mentioned above ; namely, (*a*) comparative religion, and (*b*) historical theology.

(*a*) Comparative religion is the classification and comparison of different religions or of different forms of the same religion. Its aim is to determine the precise beliefs of such and such a people or sect. It is therefore on the one hand anthropological, as involving the comparison of different human types, and on the other psychological, as determining the religious beliefs of this or that individual considered as a member of a certain class, sect, or nation. Comparative religion or religious anthropology is therefore not really to be distinguished from the Psychology of Religion.

If we ask what constitutes psychology and dis-tinguishes it from other sciences, we cannot answer merely that psychology is the study of the mind or soul. The philosophical sciences,—logic, ethics, and so forth,—attempt to study the mind ; and they are not psychological. Nor can we say (as some psychologists say) that this is the reason of their unsatisfactory character ; for these sciences exist on their own basis, and it is no criticism of one science to point out that it is not a different one. Again, we cannot define psychology as the study of conduct ; because that title is already claimed by ethics. From these philosophical sciences psychology is distinguished not by its subject but by its method.

The method peculiar to psychology may perhaps be described as follows. The psychology of knowing differs from logic or the philosophical theory of knowledge in that it treats a judgment—the act of knowing something—as an event in the mind, a historical fact. It does not go on to determine the relation of this mental event to the " something " known, the reality beyond the act[1] which the mind, in that act, apprehends. Such a further investigation would be metaphysical in character and is therefore avoided by psychology. Now this formula can be universalised, and thus gives us the definition of psychological method. Take the mental activity as a self-contained fact ; refuse, so far as that is possible, to treat of its metaphysical aspect, its relations with real things other than itself ; and you have psychology. Thus in scientific thought as studied by logic we have a judgment in which the mind knows reality : psychology, treating the judgment as a mere event, omits its reference to reality, that is to say, does not raise the question whether it is true.[2] In religion, we have people holding definite beliefs as to the nature of God. Psychology studies and classifies those beliefs without asking how far they correspond with the real nature of God. In conduct generally we have certain actions, individual or social, designed to attain the ends of morality, utility, or the like ; psychology will study

[1] The description of judgment as a mental event or act which refers to a reality beyond the act is borrowed from Mr. F. H. Bradley's *Logic*. I use Mr. Bradley's language not because I entirely accept such a description of the judgment, but because I believe it to express the view on which psychology is based ; and therefore psychology cannot be defined without reference to it.
[2] The same omission or abstraction is made by Formal Logic, which I take to be a psychological rather than a philosophical science.

these actions without asking whether they are right or wrong, but taking them merely as things done. In general, the characteristic of psychology is the refusal to raise ultimate questions. And since that is so, it is plainly not in a position to offer answers to them : or rather, in so far as it does offer answers these rest on an uncritical and quite accidental attitude towards the problems. For instance, the psychology of religion, consisting as it does in the collection of beliefs about God without determining their truth, evidently does not aim at discovering what God is and which opinions give the best account of his nature. The psychology of religion, therefore, unlike the philosophy of religion, is not itself a religion ; that is, it has no answer of its own to the question " What is God ? " It has, in fact, deliberately renounced the investigation of that question and substituted the other question, " What do different people say about him ? "

Of course a religious psychologist may be willing to offer an answer of his own to the first question. But in so far as he does that he is abandoning the psychology of religion and falling back on religion itself; changing his attitude towards religion from an external to an internal one. When I describe the attitude of psychology as " external " my meaning is this. There is an air of great concreteness and reality about psychology which makes it very attractive. But this concreteness is really a delusion and on closer inspection vanishes. When a man makes a statement about the nature of God (or anything else) he is interested, not in the fact that he is making that statement, but in the belief, or hope, or fancy that it is true. If then the psychologist merely makes a note of the statement and declines to join in the question whether it is true, he is cutting himself off from any kind of real sympathy or participation in the very thing he is studying—this man's mental life and experiences. To take an example, a certain mystic says, " God is a circle whose centre is everywhere and whose circumference is nowhere." The psychologist, instead of answering, "Of course," or, "Really?" or, "I don't quite see what you mean," replies, "That is an example of what I call the Religious Paradox."[1]

The mind, regarded in this external way, really ceases to be a mind at all. To study a man's consciousness without studying the thing of which he is conscious is not knowledge of anything, but barren and trifling abstraction. It cannot answer ultimate questions, because it has renounced the attempt ; it cannot enter into the life it studies, because it refuses to look with it eye to eye ; and it is left with the cold unreality of thought which is the thought of nothing, action with no purpose, and fact with no meaning.

These objections against the ideal of religious psychology or of the science of comparative religion only hold good so long as, from such collections of opinions, the philosophical impulse towards the determination of their truth is completely excluded. And the fact that this impulse is never really absent is what gives religious value to such studies. Indeed, this impulse alone gives them scientific value ; for some degree of critical or sympathetic understanding is necessary before the bare facts can be correctly reported. It is notorious that the unintelligent observer cannot even observe. It is only owing to surreptitious or unconscious aberrations from its ideal of "objectivity" that psychology ever accomplishes anything at all.

(b) The ideal of a history of the Church as a substitute for philosophical theology is plainly open to the same general objections. It profits nothing to catalogue the heresies of early Christianity and get them off by heart, unless; one enters with some degree of sympathy into the problems which men wished to solve, and tries to comprehend the motives which led them to offer their various answers. But this sympathy and understanding are purely religious, theological,

----

[1] This instance is not imaginary.

philosophical ; to understand a heresy one must appreciate the difficulty which led to it ; and that difficulty, however expressed, is always a philosophical difficulty. The merely external history of dogma killeth ; it is the internal history—the entering into the development of thought—that maketh alive.

The same applies, again, to the origins of Christianity. The " historical Jesus " can never solve the problem of Christianity, because there never was a " historical " Jesus pure and simple ; the real Jesus held definite beliefs about God and himself and the world ; his interest was not historical but theological. By considering him as a mere fact in history, instead of also an idea in theology, we may be simplifying our task, but we are cutting ourselves off from any true understanding and sharing of his consciousness. Historical theology is always tempted to lose itself in the merely external task of showing what formulæ he took over from current religion, and what he added to them, and what additions and alterations were superadded by the early Church ; whereas all this is but the outward aspect of the reality, and the true task of historical theology is to find out not only what was said, but what was meant ; what current Judaism, to begin with, meant by its formulæ, and how far its meaning was a satisfactory theology. Then we should be in a position to understand from within the new doctrines of Jesus, and really to place ourselves at the fountain-head of the faith. To speak of studying the mind of Jesus from within may seem presumptuous ; but no other method is of the slightest value.

2. Historical positivism thus fails to give any answer to theological questions. It can tell us that the Church has anathematised certain doctrines. But what those doctrines mean, or why any one ever held them, or what the Church meant to assert by condemning them, or even why it follows that we ought to condemn them too, pure history can never tell us.

For the solution of these problems we are thrown back on speculative thought.

Hence, through condemnation of the over-emphasis laid on historical truth, emerges a contrary theory : namely, that history is useless as a basis for theology. This anti-historical view may take two forms : (*a*) that history is itself too uncertain to bear such an important superstructure as theology ; (*b*) that the two things are truths of different orders, so that one cannot have any bearing on the other.

(*a*) However well attested a historical fact may be, it is never more than merely attested. It is always possible that it may be wrong ; we have no means of checking it ; it is always conceivable that evidence might turn up sufficient to discredit the best established historical belief. And — still worse — the evidence might never turn up, and we should simply go on believing what was totally untrue. Seeing, then, how desperately uncertain history must always be, can we, dare we, use it as the foundation for all our creeds ?

This argument introduces a new form of scepticism, which we may describe as anti-historical scepticism. It is in essence a statement of the unknowability of past fact simply as such, on the abstract ground that failure of memory, breach of the tradition, is always possible. This is entirely parallel to the anti-philosophical scepticism which declares that no inference is sound because of the unavoidable abstract possibility of a logical fallacy. Each is a fantastic and hypercritical position, and neither is really tenable. If inference as such is to be distrusted, the evidence that leads us to distrust it is discredited with the rest. If attested fact as such is liable to be misreported, the facts on which we base this generalisation are as doubtful as any others. Indeed the theory puts a stop to every kind of activity ; for if the human memory as such is the seat of the supposed fallacy, we cannot count upon any continuity whatever in our mental

life ; it may always be the case that my memory of
five minutes ago is completely misleading.   If I may
not base a theory on facts reported in books of history,
am I more entitled to trust those recollected by
myself ?   Plainly there is no difference of kind here.
But if the sceptic falls back on a question of degree
and says that some facts are better attested than others,
then of course one agrees with him and admits that
one is always bound to ask whether these facts are
well enough attested to serve as basis for this theory ;
whether the facts are two thousand years or two
minutes distant in time makes no real difference.

(*b*) The other argument against the use of history
in theology asserts that there are two categories of fact,
historical and philosophical ; and that since they are
totally distinct, theological propositions, which are
essentially philosophical in character, cannot be proved
or disproved or in the least affected by historical
arguments ; just as discussions about the authorship
of a poem do not in the least affect its beauty.

This argument is plainly right if it merely means
that you cannot as if by magic extract a philosophical
conclusion from non-philosophical premisses.   If you
understand history as something entirely excluding
philosophical elements, then any philosophical conclusion which you "prove" by its means will be
dishonestly gained.   But in this sense the statement
is no more than the tautology that you cannot extract
from an argument more than its premisses contain ;
it does not help us to recognise a purely historical or
philosophical argument when we meet one, or even
convince us that such things exist.

It may, secondly, be interpreted to mean that when
we cite instances in support of philosophical views the
philosophical conclusion depends not on the historical
fact but on the "construction," as it is called, which we
put upon the fact.   We look at the fact in the light of
an idea ; and the philosophical theory which we describe

as proved by the fact is due not to the fact but to the idea we have read into it. Here again there is a certain truth. When A finds his pet theory of human selfishness borne 'out by C's action, and B uses the same action as an illustration of his own theory of human altruism, it seems natural to say that each starts from the same fact but with different preconceived ideas : and that the fact is really equally irrelevant to both the theories which it is used to prove. But this account of the matter is quite inaccurate. A's " idea " is that C's act was a selfish act ; B's " idea " was that it was altruistic. But of these ideas neither was a mere " idea " ; one was a historical fact and the other a historical error. Thus the distinction between the fact and the construction put upon it is false ; what we call the construction is only our attempt to determine further details about the fact. And since the question whether C was acting selfishly or not is a question of historical fact, the doctrine that people act in general selfishly or altruistically is based entirely on historical fact, or on something erroneously imagined to be historical fact. The attempt to dissociate philosophy and history breaks down because, in point of fact, we never do so dissociate them. One simply cannot make general statements without any thought of their instances.

3. Positivism and scepticism both break down under examination. We cannot, it appears, do without either philosophical or historical thought. We seem therefore to have here a distinction within the region of the intellect parallel to that of intellect and will in the mind as a whole ; and consequently we must investigate the relation between philosophy and history with a view to determining as accurately as possible the nature of the distinction.

(a) In the first place, it appears that history cannot exist without philosophy. There is no such thing as an entirely non-philosophical history. History cannot proceed without philosophical presuppositions of a highly

complex character. It deals with evidence, and therefore makes epistemological assumptions as to the value
of evidence ; it describes the actions of historical characters in terms whose meaning is fixed by ethical
thought ; it has continually to determine what events
are possible and what are not possible, and this can
only be done in virtue of some general metaphysical
conclusions.

It is not, of course, implied that no historian is
qualified for his work without a systematic education
in academic philosophy. Still less is it to be supposed
that a philosopher dabbling in history is better able
than the historians to lay down the law as to the value
of such and such a historical argument. It must be
remembered that by philosophy we mean, here as elsewhere, thought concerned with metaphysical problems :
not acquaintance with technical literature and the
vocabulary of the specialist.

(*b*) It is equally certain that philosophy is impossible
without history ; for any theory must be a theory of
facts, and if there were no facts there would be no
occasion for theory. But in asserting the necessity of
history to philosophy we must guard against certain
misunderstandings.

In the first place, the above statement may be interpreted to mean that philosophy develops or evolves
along fixed lines, has a definite history of its own in
the sense of a movement in which each phase emerges
necessarily from the preceding phase, and therefore
philosophy (*i.e.* the state of philosophical thought now)
depends absolutely upon history (*i.e.* its own previous
history).

As against such a view it must be pointed out that
philosophy is a human activity, not a mechanical
process ; and is therefore free and not in any sense
necessitated either by its own past or anything else.
Doubtless every philosopher owes much to his predecessors ; thought is a corporate activity, like every

other.   But the dependence of Hegel upon Kant, say,
is of quite a different kind from the dependence indicated by the above theory.   Hegel's work is based
upon Kant, in the sense that many of Kant's truths are
Hegel's truths too ; but Kant also makes errors which
Hegel corrects.   The error is not the basis of the truth
but the opposite of it.   It may, and indeed in a sense
must, lead to it ; because an error cannot be refuted till
it has been stated.   But the statement of the error is
not the *cause* of its refutation.   The word " cause " is
simply inapplicable ; for we are dealing with the free
activity of the mind, not with a mechanical process.
And therefore this theory uses the word dependence in
a misleading sense.

Secondly, philosophy may be said to depend on
history in the sense that history, the gradual and
cumulative experience of facts, is necessary before we
can frame philosophical theories on a broad enough
basis.   The wider a man's experience, the more likely
his generalisations are to be true.   The same applies to
the human race in general ; we have been accumulating
facts little by little for centuries now, and consequently
we are a great deal better equipped for philosophising
than were, for instance, the Greeks.

This theory expresses a point of view which is
always widely held ; it is an attitude towards the world
whose technical name is empiricism, and of which the
dominant note is the abstract insistence on mere number
or size.   It reckons wisdom by the quantity of different
things a man knows, and certainty by the number of
different times a statement comes true ; it holds that a
man broadens his views by travelling, and stunts them
by living at home ; it measures everything in two
dimensions, and forgets the existence of a third.   As
a matter of fact—one is almost ashamed of having to
utter such truisms—he who accumulates information
alone is very likely to accumulate not merely sorrow
but indigestion of the mind ; if he cannot understand

himself, he is not necessarily the wiser for trying to understand others ; if he cannot learn truth at home, he will certainly not learn it abroad. It is true that more facts of some kinds are known to the learned world now than in the time of Socrates ; but it does not follow that we are all wiser than Socrates. The notion of establishing theories on a broad basis is, in short, an error ; itself based upon a broad, but extremely superficial, theory of logic. What matters in the foundations of a theory is not their breadth but their depth ; the thorough understanding of a single fact, not the feverish accumulation of a thousand.

History must be regarded not as a mechanical process, nor yet as a gradual accumulation of truths, but simply as *objectivity* ; as the real fact of which we are conscious. History is that which actually exists; fact, as something independent of my own or your knowledge of it. In this sense there would be no philosophy without it ; for no form of consciousness can exist without an object. We are not expelling from history the notion of movement ; for if we are asked, what is the nature of this reality of which we are conscious ? we shall reply that it is itself activity, growth, development ; but not development in any automatic or mechanical sense.

4. We are now able to suggest more fully the relation of history to philosophy. Neither can exist without the other ; each presupposes the other. That is to say, they are interdependent and simultaneous activities, like thought and will. The question is whether, like thought and will, they are fully identical.

Each is knowledge ; and if they are different, they must be the knowledge of different objects. How can we distinguish these objects ? History, it is sometimes said, is knowledge of the particular, philosophy knowledge of the universal. But the particular is no mere particular ; it is a particular of this or that universal ; and the universal never can exist at all except in the form of this or that particular. " The universal " and

E

" the particular " considered as separate concrete things
are fictions ; and to equate the distinction of philosophy
and history with such a fictitious distinction is to admit
at once that it is untenable.

Nor can we distinguish them as the knowledge of
the necessary and of the contingent respectively. This
distinction is due to the fact that a theory explains
some things but leaves others unexplained ; and this
remnant, relatively to the theory, appears as " the
contingent." Contingent, therefore, is only a synonym
for unexplained ; it cannot mean inexplicable, for if
there is a sense in which anything is explicable, we
cannot assume that anything is in this sense not
explicable. In the last resort necessary probably means
no more than real : when we say that a thing is
necessarily so, we mean that we understand it to be
really so. And therefore whatever is real is necessarily real. In point of fact, it is possible that the
distinction between necessity and contingence is only
a restatement of that between the universal and the
particular.

It would, again, be a repetition of the same idea if
we tried to distinguish things that happen in time
(history) from things that are true independently of
time (philosophy). For there is one sense in which
every truth is temporal ; as for instance the nature of
God is historically revealed, and the fact that twice two
is four is grasped by adding, on a definite occasion,
two and two ; and there is another sense in which
every fact is independent of time ; as it is still true and
always will be true that the battle of Hastings was
fought in 1066. The difference between a temporal
event and a timeless truth is a difference not between
two different classes of thing, but between two aspects
of the same thing. This attempt to distinguish philosophy and history suggests a dualism between two
complete worlds ; the one unchanging, self-identical,
and known by philosophy, the other subject to change

and development, and known by history. But a world of mere self-identity would be as inconceivable as a world of mere change ; each quality is the reverse side of the other. To separate the two is to destroy each alike.

History, like philosophy, is the knowledge of the one real world ; it is historical, that is, subject to the limitation of time, because only that is known and done which has been known and done ; the future, not being mechanically determined, does not yet exist, and therefore is no part of the knowable universe. It is philosophical, that is, all-embracing, universal, for the same reason ; because historical fact is the only thing that exists and includes the whole universe. History *a parte objecti*—the reality which historical research seeks to know—is nothing else than the totality of existence ; and this is also the object of philosophy. History *a parte subjecti*—the activity of the historian—is investigation of all that has happened and is happening ; and this is philosophy too. For it is incorrect to say that philosophy is theory *based upon* fact ; theory is not something else derived, distilled, from facts but simply the observation that the facts are what they are. And similarly the philosophical presuppositions of history are not something different from the history itself : they are philosophical truths which the historian finds historically exemplified.

History and philosophy are therefore the same thing. It is true, no doubt, that each in turn may be interpreted abstractly ; abstract history being the mere verbal description of events without any attempt at understanding them, philosophy the dry criticism of formal rules of thinking without any attempt at grasping their application. Abstract history in this sense is a failure not because it is unphilosophical, but because it is unhistorical ; it is not really history at all. And similarly abstract philosophy becomes meaningless, because in eliminating the historical element it has unawares eliminated the philosophical element too. Each alike must also be the other or it cannot be itself; each in being itself is also the other.

5. The value of historical theology, then, consists in the fact that it is already philosophical. It does not merely supply philosophical theology with materials; it is itself already grappling with the philosophical problems. Religion cannot afford to ignore its historical content, nor can it treat this content as something inessential to the establishment of its speculative doctrines. History must bear the weight of speculative superstructure to the best of its ability; but in return it may derive help from philosophical light thrown thereby on its own difficulties. In this way the distinction between philosophical and historical theology disappears; there is seen to be only one theology, which is both these at once. It may be presented with comparative emphasis on constructive doctrine, as in the later chapters of this book; but if so, it does not omit or ignore history. It is woven of strands each of which is historical in character, and the whole presents itself as a historical fact. Similarly, theology may be written from a historical point of view, with the emphasis on temporal development; but it is only theology so long as it is clear that the thing that is developing is really doctrine all the time.

An illustration may serve to indicate the necessity to theology of its historical aspect. In view of the criticisms often brought against the records of the life of Jesus, many are inclined to take up a sceptical attitude and to declare that our tradition is hopelessly incorrect. But, they go on to ask, what then? We learn many valuable lessons from the Good Samaritan, though we do not believe him to have existed. We learn, too, from Homer, even if Homer never wrote what we ascribe to him. We have the tradition in black and white; it bears its credentials on its face; all else is a side-issue. Is there anything we learn from

the Christ-history that we could not equally learn from
the Christ-myth ?

The simple religious mind would, I believe, emphatically reject such a suggestion. And this would be
perfectly right. It is easy to say that the " Christ-
myth " embodies facts about God's nature which, once
known, are known whether they are learnt from one
source or from another. That is by no means the
whole truth. The life of Christ gives us, conspicuously,
two other things. It gives us an example of how a
human life may satisfy the highest possible standards ;
and it puts us in contact with the personality of
the man who lived that life.

The whole value of an example is lost unless it is
historical. If an athlete tries to equal the feats of
Herakles, or an engineer spends his life trying to
recover the secret of the man who invented a perpetual-
motion machine, they are merely deluding themselves
with false hopes if Herakles and the supposed inventor
never lived. The Good Samaritan's action is the kind
of thing that any good man might do ; it is typical of
a kind of conduct which we see around us and know
to be both admirable and possible. But if the life of
Jesus is a myth, it is more preposterous to ask a man
to imitate it than to ask him to imitate Herakles.
Any valid command must guarantee the possibility of
carrying it out ; and the historical life of Jesus is the
guarantee that man can be perfect if he will.

Further, in that perfection, or the struggle towards
it, the religious man somehow feels that he is in
personal touch with a risen Christ. We do not at
present demand an explanation of this feeling, or ask
whether there is a real intercourse ; it is enough that
the feeling exists and is an integral part of the Christian
consciousness. The presence of Christ is as real to the
believer as the love of God. But it can hardly be real
if Christ is a myth.

It must be observed that we are not arguing to the

reality of Christ's presence now, or his historicity in the past, on the strength of this feeling. Such an argument would be extremely hazardous. We are merely concerned to show that Christianity would not be absolutely unchanged by the demonstration that these things were mythical. The belief that Christ really lived, whether it is true or false, colours the whole consciousness of the believer.

The same holds good even of purely "intellectual" doctrine. If a doctrine is simple and easy, containing nothing very new or paradoxical, a fiction is enough to drive it home. But if it is difficult to grasp and conflicts with our preconceived notions, our first impulse is to challenge the reality of the fact which serves as an instance. A scientist propounds some new and revolutionary doctrine; at once we ask whether the experiments on which it is based were fairly carried out as he describes them. If not, we dismiss the doctrine. No doubt to an absolutely perfect mind a fiction would be as illuminating as a fact, because *ex hypothesi* such a mind would have no special difficulty in grasping any truth, however subtle, and would stand in no need of, so to speak, forcible conviction. A person who was the equal or superior of Jesus Christ in spiritual insight could give up his historicity and not lose by it. But such a description only applies to God. And in God, we can no longer distinguish between the historical and the imaginary. If, speaking in a Platonic myth, we describe the course of history as a story told to himself by God, it makes no difference whether we say the story is imaginary or true.

But for us objective fact, history, is necessary. We all have something of the spirit of Thomas, and must know a thing has happened before we can believe its teaching. Is this, perhaps, one reason for the difference between the parables that Jesus spoke and the parable he acted? He knew the limitations of his audience ;

he saw what they could understand and what they could not. Some things about God he could tell them in words, and they would believe his words ; but one last thing—how could he tell that ? and if he could find words to tell it, who would not mock him for a visionary or shrink from him as a blasphemer ?   There was only one way ; to act the parable he could not speak.   We are accustomed to think of the death of Jesus as the sacrifice for our sins. Was it not also, perhaps, a sacrifice for our stupidity ?

PART II

RELIGION AND METAPHYSICS

CHAPTER I

1. It might be maintained that the first duty of a philosophical theology, indeed of any theology, is to prove the existence of the God whose nature it professes to expound. The difficulty of this preliminary task is so great that theology tries in general to escape it ; pointing out that every science starts from some data, some fact taken for granted. The physicist is not called upon to prove the existence of matter, nor the historian to prove the existence of his documentary authorities. Granted that matter exists, the physicist will tell you what it is like ; and theology must claim to exercise the same freedom in the choice of a starting-point.

(a) This defence is in part justified, and in part, I think, mistaken. It may be true that no empirical science would submit its foundations to such rigorous criticism as is here applied to theology. And if theology is to be a merely empirical science, it has a corresponding right to make uncriticised assumptions. But the sting of the criticism lies in the fact that theology claims to be more than this. It presents itself as a philosophy, a view of the universe as a whole, the ultimate ground of reality ; and philosophy can take nothing for granted. A historian may say, " I give you here a sketch of the character of Julius Cæsar. It is based on all the available evidence ; but though I have weighed the documents as well as I could, and allowed for the

partisanship of one writer and the prejudice of another,
I still feel that the evidence is very slight and scanty,
and that no high degree of certainty is possible. We
have to remember in dealing with remote history that
no proof of a statement can ever be offered which will
stand against the objections of a determined scepticism."
If a theologian prefaced his account of the nature of
God by a statement in terms analogous to these, he
would doubtless win the approval of many for his
toleration and breadth of mind; but all sincerely
religious people would, I am convinced, feel that his
detached and judicial attitude was not merely an outrage
on their feelings but exhibited a certain intellectual
obtuseness and incapacity to appreciate the point at
issue. We should have the same feeling if a philosopher
said, "Such, in my opinion, is the nature of morality.
We must not, however, forget that some people deny
the existence of morality altogether, and it is quite
possible that they are right." To such language we
should reply that a philosopher has no right to construct
the nature of morality out of his inner consciousness,
and end in the pious hope that the reality may correspond with his "ideal construction." His business as
a philosopher is to discover what actually are the ideals
which govern conduct, and not to speak until he has
something to tell us about them. In the same way, the
theologian's business is to understand, at least in some
degree, the nature of God; if he cannot claim to do
this, he has no claim on our attention. A hypothetical
science, one which says, "These are the characteristics of
matter, or number, or space, granted that such things
really exist"—may be incomplete, but it is at any rate
something; a hypothetical philosophy or theology is
not merely mutilated but destroyed.

If we say to a scientist, "First prove to me that
matter exists, and then I will hear what you have to say
about it," he will answer, "That is metaphysics, and I
have nothing to do with it." But theology is already

metaphysical through and through ; so it would appear that when we say to a theologian " I must have proof that God exists before I can be expected to listen to your description of him," the theologian is bound to supply the proof, and his science must stand still until he has done it. But this is at least not what theologians actually do ; and though it may be replied that none the less they ought to do it, is the demand quite fair either to them or to the scientists ?

(b) The scorn with which the scientist utters the word " metaphysics " shows that he does not think the worse of physics for refusing to embark upon the arguments so entitled. And yet surely the physicist cannot suppose that it makes no difference to physics whether matter exists or not. Nor is it strictly true to say, as is often said, that he assumes matter to exist; that is to say, begs the metaphysical question in his own favour. His real position is quite different from this. " How can I prove the existence of a thing " (he might say) " whose nature is totally undefined ? Did Newton first prove to a mystified world the existence of fluxions, and only afterwards deign to explain what he meant by the word ? If you will listen to me and hear what I have got to say about matter, you can then go on to criticise it, that is, to ask whether the thing which I call matter really exists. But this metaphysics, arguing about the reality or unreality of a thing you have never tried to describe, seems to me a waste of time."

(c) The theologian, I think, ought to put in the same plea. A proof of the existence of God is all very well, but there are " Gods many," if by God you understand whatever this or that man happens to mean by the word. Would a proof of the existence of God prove that Apollo and Hathor and Krishna and Mumbo Jumbo all existed ? and if so, what becomes of any religion, if every other is exactly as true ? Plainly, if the God of one religion exists, the God of a contradictory religion cannot exist ; and the proof of one is the disproof of

the other.   Let us first determine what we mean by
God, and then and only then we can profitably ask
whether he exists.

This second demand is more reasonable than the
first ; but it still has one grave defect.   The determination of what I believe (about God or about anything
else) is not a different thing from the question whether
that belief is true.   To believe a thing is to regard it
as true ; and to attach a meaning to a word, to believe
that this and no other is the right meaning, is to assert
that the thing which you so name exists, and exists in
this form and no other.   Nor can we escape this conclusion by quoting the time-honoured instance of the
dragon, in which, it is supposed, we attach a meaning
to a word without believing that the thing so named
really exists ; for dragons do exist in Fairyland, and it
is only in Fairyland that the word has any meaning.

To attach a meaning to a word, then, is to claim
that this meaning is the right one : that is, that the
thing whose name it is really exists, and that this is its
actual nature.   To distinguish between the question,
" What do I mean by God ? " and the question, " Does
God exist, and if so what is he like ? " is impossible, for
the two questions are one and the same.   It is, of
course, possible to distinguish the meaning I attach to
the word, or my conception of God, from another
person's meaning or conception ; and it may be possible,
comparing these two, to discover which is the better
and to adopt it.   But in any case, the statement of
what we mean by God (or anything else) is not the
mere expression of a " subjective idea " or of the "meaning of a word " as distinct from the "nature of a thing."
It is already critical, so far as we have the power of
making it so ; it presupposes that we have reasons for
believing that idea, that meaning, to be the right one.

Thus the proof of the existence of God is not
something else without which theology is incomplete ;
it is theology itself.   The reasoned statement of the

attributes of God is at the same time the proof that the
God who has those attributes is the God who exists.
Similarly, physics does not require to be supplemented
by a metaphysical proof that matter exists ; it already
supplies that proof in the form of an answer to the
question, " What conception of matter is the right
conception ? "

It may be objected to this way of putting it that
the existence of matter in the one case and God in the
other really has been dogmatically assumed : and that
thus we are falling into the very error which we set out
to avoid.   This is not the case.   The assumption that
some form of matter exists is only an assumption if a
meaning is already attached to the word matter ; and
since to supply the meaning is the function of physics,
the word cannot mean anything at the outset.   Actually,
of course, this vacuum of meaning never exists, because
the science is never at its absolute starting-point ; each
new scientist begins with the meaning conferred on the
word by his predecessors.   But does he therefore assume
that matter exists in a form precisely corresponding to
that meaning ?   If so, it would indeed be a monstrous
assumption.   But he does not.   If he did, he would
not be a scientist.   His whole function as a scientist is
to ask whether the matter conceived by his predecessors
exists at all.   He may discover that their conception
was radically false, in which case there is no limit to
the degree of change which the meaning of the word
" matter " will undergo in his hands.

The answer to the question what we mean by the
word God, then, is identical with that to the question
whether God exists.   " What do we mean by the word
God ? " resolves itself into the question, " What is the
right meaning to attach to the word ? " and that again
is indistinguishable from the question, " What sort of
God exists ? "   To suppose that this doctrine rules out
atheism is merely to misunderstand it ; for it might
quite well be that the word God, like the word dragon,

means something which exists only in the realm of the imagination.

It follows that we shall not begin by proving the existence of God, nor indeed offer any formal proof at all. But this is not because the existence of God cannot, in the nature of things, be proved. It is often maintained that ultimate truths are incapable of proof, and that the existence of God is such an ultimate truth. But I venture to suggest that the impossibility of proof attaches not to ultimate truths as such, but only to the truths of " metaphysics " in the depreciatory sense of the word ; to truths, that is, which have no definite meaning. We cannot prove that Reality exists, not because the question is too " ultimate " (that is, because too much depends on it), but because it is too empty. Tell us what you mean by Reality, and we can offer an alternative meaning and try to discover which is the right one. No one can prove that God exists, if no definite significance is attached to the words ; not because—as is doubtless the case—the reality of God transcends human knowledge, but because the idea of God which we claim to have is as yet entirely indeterminate. In the same way, we cannot prove or disprove the existence of matter until we know what sort of matter is meant ; but something can certainly be done to prove the existence or non-existence of the matter of Democritus or Gassendi or Clerk Maxwell.

I do not wish to imply that hesitation and diffidence are mistaken attitudes in which to approach these questions. There is a false mystery, which consists in the asking of unreasonable and unanswerable questions ; but there is also a true mystery, which is to be found everywhere and supremely in that which is the centre and sum of all existence. In approaching these hardest of all problems, only the most short-sighted will expect to find their full solution, and only the least discriminating will think at the end that he has found it. Herein lies the real ground for humility ; not that our faculties exhaust themselves in a vain struggle to compass the unknowable, but that however well we do we have never done all we might or all we could ; and are, after all, unprofitable servants of the supreme wisdom.

2. The common charge of inconclusiveness brought against the traditional proofs of God's existence is thus to a certain extent justified ; for these proofs are, in their usual forms, isolated arguments, detached from any positive theology and attempting to demonstrate the existence of a God whose nature is very vaguely conceived. This fact is sometimes expressed by saying that they are purely negative. It would be better to say that they are highly abstract, and that a full statement of any one of them would amount to the construction of a complete theological metaphysic. No argument can be purely negative, for it is impossible to deny one principle except by asserting another, however little that other is explicitly developed.

(a) But there is another charge often brought against these proofs, which relates less to their positive value than to the temper in which they are conceived. It is supposed that they are the fruit not of free speculation but of an illicit union between dogmatism and philosophy, authority and criticism. They are believed to be typical of a benighted period when ecclesiastical tradition fixed not only the limits but the very conclusions of metaphysical thought ; when reason was so debased as to submit to accepting its results blindly at the hands of an unquestioned dogmatism, and to demean itself to the task, apologetic in the worst sense, of bolstering up by sophistical ingenuity these uncriticised beliefs.

This view of the traditional proofs, though popular at the present time, is neither historical nor fully reasonable. The Middle Ages were undoubtedly a period when the authority of the Church counted for much ; but these proofs are so far from being typically mediæval

F

that they run, in one form or another, through the whole of philosophy. If the history of speculation begins with Socrates, Socrates was the first person known to us who definitely formulated the Argument from Design ; and Socrates was no blind supporter of dogma. The Ontological proof, first I believe clearly stated by the sceptical philosopher Sextus Empiricus in refutation of the reckless dogmatism of contemporary atheists, enters modern philosophy indeed with Anselm in the Middle Ages, but was not accepted by the orthodox scholastic tradition, and the recognition of its importance was left to Descartes in the full tide of the Renaissance. Since then it has never lost its place as one of the central problems of the theory of knowledge. The third traditional proof, from the contingency or imperfection of the world to some cause outside the world, is mediæval only because it was already Aristotelian, and Aristotle, whatever his shortcomings, cannot any more than Socrates be represented as an example of the priest-ridden intellect.

The objection seems to consist in the notion that a proof of some belief which is itself held on other grounds is illegitimate and insincere. Let us—so the notion runs—employ our reason in the discovery of new truths, not in the invention of proofs for truths, if truths they be, which we learnt from another source and shall continue to believe even if the proof breaks down. By the latter course we learn nothing new, even if it is successful ; we only delude ourselves into mistaking the source from which our beliefs are derived.

But this objection will not stand examination. In the first place, it would apply with equal force to the discovery of a proof in the case of, let us say, a mathematical theorem ; where we often see the thing to be true but cannot offer any proof of it. Here the discovery of a proof is subsequent to the existence of the belief, and the belief does not disappear if we fail to discover any proof at all. Why then is it desirable to prove the theorem ?

First, perhaps, in order to make sure that our original conviction was not a mere error. If we never tested our first impressions by such means, the mistakes of which we make quite enough already would be indefinitely multiplied. Secondly, in order that by means of the proof we may impart our conviction to persons less gifted than ourselves with the faculty of mathematical intuition. And thirdly, because in discovering the proof we really do attain new knowledge. Even if we do no more than make explicit the steps by which our mind leapt to its first conclusion, knowledge of our mental processes is gained ; and, moreover, no proof can be constructed without discovering new facts about the relation of this theorem to other things which we already knew. And the discovery that one truth necessitates another is a discovery worth making.

"The parallel," it may be said, "is unfair. The discovery of a proof is in this case valuable precisely because it is homogeneous with the original intuition. Each was an example of mathematical thinking, and therefore each bears on and is relevant to the other. But the belief in the existence of God is not the fruit of the same kind of thought as the formal proof of his existence. The one is passively taken on authority, the other critically constructed by the reason."

Authority does enter largely into the formation of all our beliefs, not excluding those of religion. But it is not peculiar to religion. Even in mathematics, a surveyor, an astronomer, a navigator uses countless formulæ which he has never proved and never dreams of testing. In science, the learner takes a vast proportion of his beliefs on the authority of his teacher or the writer of his handbook. It would be strange if in religion alone there were no place for authority.

(b) And it is doubtless true that there is a distinction

between believing a thing because one is told it by an expert, and believing it because one has been into the evidence for oneself. It is precisely the distinction between the man in the street and the original investigator, philosopher, physicist, mathematician, or whatever he may be. But the objection which we are considering puts a peculiar interpretation on this distinction. Because a man has once been a learner, it maintains, he cannot become an independent investigator unless he first forgets what he has learnt. If he attempts to philosophise about God, he must first cease to believe in his existence. But is this reasonable? Must we celebrate the beginning of our research into a subject by denying all we have been taught about it? "Not perhaps by denying, but certainly by questioning." Yes, no doubt : by asking whether we do believe : and, if we find we still do, by asking why we believe. Philosophy may start as well from one place as from another : and the fact that a man does actually believe in the existence of God, or of his fellow-man, or of an external material world, is no barrier to his becoming a philosopher. The modern " broad-minded " critic would have him dissimulate these convictions, if he cannot get rid of them ; and maintains that to come on the field with opinions ready made is to be hopelessly prejudiced. But the alternative, to come on the field with no opinions at all, is unfortunately impossible. It does not matter where you start, but you must start somewhere ; and to begin by making a clean sweep of all your beliefs is only to deprive yourself of all material on which to work. Or rather, since the feat can never be really accomplished, it is to put yourself at the mercy of those surreptitious beliefs and assumptions which your broom has left lurking in the darker corners.

We are dealing not with abstract ideals, but with the ways and means of ordinary life and everyday thinking. No actual man can ever claim that his mind is, thanks to his sedulous avoidance of prejudice, a

perfect and absolute blank as regards the matter he
proposes to investigate. There is only one course open
to any critic : to discover what he actually does think,
and then to find out, if he can, whether his first idea
was just or not ; that is, to prove it or to disprove it.
Systematic scepticism is the essence of all philosophy
and all science ; but scepticism, if it means pretending
not to entertain convictions which in fact one finds
inevitable, soon passes over into systematic falsehood.

Bearing in mind, then, that the preliminary statement of belief must be already, to some extent, critical,
we can see that the method of argument to which exception was taken is not only inevitable in practice,
but theoretically sound. The kind of thinking which
accepts truths on authority is not " passive," not funda-
mentally distinct from that which criticises every step
in detail. The authority is not accepted without some
reason, and the fact that it is accepted does not in-
capacitate us from analysing the reasons for acceptance
and from discovering further reasons.

3. This may serve to explain the scheme of the remaining chapters of this book. We shall not formally
lay down the Christian, or any other, theory of God and
then attempt to prove it either in itself or against alternatives. This would be both wearisome and artificial ;
for the exposition cannot be separated from the criticism.
Neither shall we attempt a metaphysical construction,
free from all presuppositions, which should demonstrate
a priori the truth of the Christian theology ; for this
would entail the same arbitrary separation of the two
things, even if it were not setting ourselves an initial
task far beyond our power.

I intend rather to state as simply as possible certain
beliefs concerning God and the world which are at
least central to the Christian theology, and then to
examine certain alternatives to these, or objections
alleged against them, which are familiar to modern
readers. In this way it may be possible to develop in

the following three chapters a general view of the nature of God ; and in the remaining part I shall apply the results so obtained to some problems which, I imagine, would be commonly described as belonging less to metaphysics than to theology. The distinction between these two spheres, however, must not be insisted upon. The problem of the Incarnation is simply that of the true nature of man and his relation to the absolute spirit ; the Atonement presents in theological terms the purely ethical question of the relation between the good will and the bad ; and the problem of Miracle is not in the last resort to be distinguished from that of the freedom of the will.

The points I wish to examine in this part are as follows. Christian theology regards God as spirit, exercising creative power, however conceived, over the world of matter. This material world is supposed truly to exist, that is, to be no mere illusion : but yet to be not self-existent but to depend for its existence and nature on will. This view brings it into conflict with materialism, which regards matter as self-existent and indeed as the only true reality. This antithesis will form the subject of the next chapter.

Secondly, God is conceived as a person ; but a person not exclusively related to other persons. His spirit—his mind—may enter into, may become an element of, indeed the very self of, a given human mind. And this is attained without loss of freedom or individuality on the part of that human mind. This paradox is in conflict with the popular view of personality as always exclusive and independent, which makes every person absolutely self-contained and autonomous : and the distinction between the Christian and this latter or individualistic theory of personality will be discussed in Chapter III.

Thirdly, God is perfectly good and yet, as omnipotent, he is the ruler or creator of a universe in which good and bad exist side by side. Christianity can give

up neither of these doctrines ; it is equally hostile to a
theism which restricts God's power, that is, makes him
only one of a number of limited or finite beings, for
the sake of preserving his goodness, and to a pantheism
which denies his goodness in the interest of his infini-
tude. This dilemma must be faced to the best of our
ability in Chapter IV.

These three inquiries do not exhaust even the leading points and difficulties in the Christian conception
of God ; but they are enough to take us into the
most perilous regions of metaphysics, where the angelic
doctors fear to tread. The problem of matter has
hardly yet been settled by the advance of philosophy :
that of personality is the subject of continual controversy : and that of evil is often given up as insoluble. We cannot expect to achieve at best more
than a partial solution of the infinite questions which
these problems raise : and that not only because philosophy still has far to go, but because it is the nature
of truth to present itself under infinite aspects and to
offer an endless variety of problems where at first only
one is seen.

CHAPTER II

POPULAR metaphysic distinguishes two categories of reality, mind and matter. Mind is a reality whose qualities are thought, will, and so forth ; it is not extended over space or divisible into parts. Matter, on the other hand, occupies space, and is homogeneously subdivisible into smaller parts ; it has no consciousness of itself as mind has, nor can it originate any train of events of its own free will. Mind is active, and acts according to its volitions ; matter is passive, and the changes in its condition, all of which are forms of motion, must be brought about either by the influence of other portions of matter, or by that of mind. Matter is thus subject to the law of causation, the law that whatever happens has a cause, external to itself, which determines it to happen in this way and in no other. This law of causation does not apply to mind, whose changes of state are initiated freely from within, in the form of acts of will. These acts of will may influence matter, but they cannot alter or in any way affect the operation of the laws which govern the movements of matter.

The importance of this distinction from our point of view is that most religions, and notably Christianity, teach a metaphysic different from this. They hold that whatever happens in the world is brought about not by automatic causation but by the free activity of one or more spirits ; and consequently they place mind not side by side with matter as a co-ordinate reality but above it. On the other hand, materialism reverses this order, ascribes everything to the operation of matter, or causation, and denies to spirit any arbitrament in the course of the world's history. We have thus three hypotheses before us. Either the world is entirely material, or it is entirely spiritual, or it is a compound of the two. When it is said that the world is "entirely" material or spiritual it is not meant that the phenomena commonly described as mind or matter are simply illusory ; it is of course allowed that they exist, but they are explained in such a way as to reduce them to the position of instances of the opposite principle. Thus materialism will admit the existence of thought, but will try to explain it as a kind of mechanism ; the opposite theory (which for the sake of convenience I shall call idealism) [1] will admit the existence of mechanism, but will try to describe it in such a way that its operation is seen to be a form of spiritual activity.

1. Of these three alternatives we shall begin by examining the most popular ; that is to say, the dualism which regards the world as composed of two different and clearly-distinguishable things, mind and matter. This theory, or some theory of the kind, may be described as the plain man's metaphysic. And as such, it has all the strength and all the weakness of an uncritical view. It is not led by a desire for unity, illegitimately satisfied, to neglect or deny one class of fact because it seems irreconcilable with another. The temper which gives every fact its full weight is necessary to any one who pretends to scientific thought ; but it is one-sided and dangerous to the

---

[1] This sense of the word must be carefully distinguished from Idealism as a theory of knowledge. The former, concerned with the antithesis between mind and matter, has no connexion whatever with the latter, which concerns the quite different antithesis of subject and object, and is opposed not to Materialism but to Realism.

truth unless balanced by its apparent opposite, the determination to draw the right conclusions from premises even if these conclusions seem to contradict the facts. Faith in facts—the belief that every fact, if correctly observed, has its own unique value—is not really antithetical, but rather identical, with the faith in reason which believes that any rightly-drawn inference is as true, as much knowledge of reality, as the observed fact from which it started. It is a common mistake to imagine that the philosopher who says, "This fact is incompatible with my theory, and therefore my theory is probably wrong," is superior in intellectual honesty to him who says, "This fact is incompatible with my theory, and therefore I must ask whether it *is* a fact." The only true intellectual honesty would lie in putting both these points of view at once. This may seem a truism; but there is a real danger of treating "facts" with so much respect that we fail to inquire into their credentials, and into the fine distinction between observed fact and inferred or imagined implication.

The plain man's dualism, then, seems to be an example of one half of this attitude without the other. It shows a genuine desire to do justice to all the facts, but fails to supply them with that interrelation apart from which it is hardly yet a theory at all. In other words, the plain man's dualism is always conscious of an unsolved problem, the problem of the relation of mind and matter; and this problem is not a mere by-product of the theory, not a detail whose final settlement is of comparatively small importance; it *is* the theory itself. Until some solution of the problem has been suggested, the dualistic theory has never been formulated. For that theory cannot be the mere statement that there are two things, mind and matter; to be a theory, it must offer some account of the way in which they are related; and that is just what it seldom if ever does.

(*a*) But a theory which has not solved all its difficulties—even one which has not solved the most elementary and conspicuous of them—may still be practically useful, and may indeed contain a certain amount of philosophical truth. It remains to be seen, therefore, whether dualism has these advantages. In the first place, it may be represented as a working hypothesis, if no more ; a method of classifying the sciences and of distinguishing two broad types— sciences of matter and sciences of mind. Such a distinction is a matter of convenience, whether it does or does not represent a metaphysical truth ; and we must ask whether from this point of view the distinction is of value.

Considered as a working hypothesis, it is almost painfully evident that the distinction between matter and mind does not work. The division of sciences into those of mind and those of matter does not give satisfaction to the practical scientist ; it baulks and hinders, rather than helps, his actual work. A few examples will perhaps make this clear.

If we take the case of biology, we find a remarkable instance of an entire province of knowledge claimed on the one hand by mechanists in the name of the material sciences, and on the other by vitalists old and new in the interest of the sciences of mind. The former point out that the essence of all vital functions is contained in the facts studied by bio-physics and bio-chemistry, and they further maintain that there is no ultimate distinction between bio-physics or bio-chemistry and physics or chemistry in general ; material substances are not absolved from the operation of their normal laws because for the time being they happen to be parts of an organism. The vitalists, on the other hand, assert that no kind of machine whose operation was limited by the nexus of cause and effect could possibly behave as a living body behaves. We are not concerned to ask which side is in the right ; the point is merely that to the question "Is an organism mind or matter?" biologists have no unanimous answer ready. And this is enough to show that the methods actually used in biology, the existence and progress of the science, do not absolutely depend on an answer being given. That is to say, the practical scientist so far from finding dualism a help to his work finds that it creates new difficulties, and therefore he simply ignores it.

A still more curious case is that of empirical psychology, where the functions of the mind itself are treated by methods which have been developed in connexion with the sciences of matter. Mind, according to these methods, is treated exactly as if it were matter; and psychologists claim that by these methods they have solved or can solve problems with which the philosophy of mind has for ages grappled in vain.

We need not ask whether these claims are justified; whether psychology is, as some believe, a new and brilliantly successful method of determining the true nature of mind, or whether as others maintain it is only an old fallacy in a new guise. It is enough for our present purpose to point out that it exists; that the distinction proposed by dualism as a working hypothesis is not actually accepted as helpful by the scientific men for whose benefit it is propounded.

Nor is it possible for dualism to step in and prevent these things, by compelling each method to keep to its own side of the line and prosecute trespassers. The difficulty is that the distinction between mind and matter, which seems so clear to the plain man, vanishes precisely according to his increase of knowledge about either. Until he has studied physics, physiology, psychology, he thinks he knows the difference; but as soon as he comes to grips with the thing, he is compelled to alter his opinion. The plain man in fact bases his dualism on a claim to knowledge far more sweeping than that made by any scientist, and indeed the knowledge which the plain man claims seems actually to contradict the scientist's most careful and mature judgment.

(*b*) Nor can we entirely pass over the difficulty of the relations between mind and matter, even though we have been warned in advance that the theory does not undertake to solve this problem. For it does, as commonly held, make certain statements about their relations. It holds that mind can know matter, that it can move matter by an act of will, and that it is somehow connected with a piece of matter known as the body of that particular mind ; also that matter by its motions can produce certain effects in mind, for instance, pleasure and pain, derangement and death. These are merely examples ; it matters little what examples we choose.

But is it really so easy to conceive how two things, defined in the way in which we have defined matter and mind, can act on each other? Matter can only operate in one way, namely, by moving ; and all motion in matter is caused either by impact or by attraction or repulsion ; influences exerted in either case by another piece of matter.[1] If therefore mind influences matter, that is to say, moves it, it can only do so by impinging on it or attracting it. But we do not associate these powers with mind as ordinarily conceived. They can (we should say) only belong to a thing which is spacial, possesses mass, and is capable of motion. Therefore mind cannot affect matter in any way in which matter can be affected, unless mind has properties characteristic of matter itself. That is to say, only matter can affect matter : mind can only affect matter if mind is itself material.

Can matter then influence mind? clearly not ; for its influence consists in causing motion, and this it can

---

[1] Attempts have been made to reduce the cause of all motion to impact ; but these have, I believe, never been entirely successful, and are quite foreign to modern physics. Nor are they of much value as a simplification ; for if the origin of motion by gravitation and by the attraction and repulsion of electric charges is hard to understand, its communication by impact is, properly considered, no less so ; though we have no space here to develop in detail the obscurities involved in the conception.

only do in something capable of motion, something spacial ; that is, in matter. The two halves of the universe go each its own way, each alike uninfluenced by the other. Mind cannot, by an act of will, move a piece of matter as I imagine that I am moving my pen ; and no change in the position of a material body can disturb, still less annihilate, the activity of a mind. The difficulty is not merely that the dualistic theory omits to explain how these things happen, or that it offers an unsatisfactory account of them ; it definitely implies that they cannot happen at all.

(c) There is still a third difficulty in connexion with the dualistic theory ; namely, the question how matter and mind are to be distinguished. At first sight this question is ridiculous ; for the whole theory consists of nothing but the clear and sharp distinction between the two. But it does not follow that this distinction is satisfactory. Matter is conceived as having one group of qualities, position and motion : mind as having a different group, thought and will. Now we distinguish two different pieces of matter by their having different positions ; and we distinguish mind from matter as a whole, presumably, by its having no position at all. But has mind really no position? If that were the case, position would be irrelevant to consciousness as it is, for instance, to time ; and my consciousness would be all over the universe precisely as 11.15 A.M. Greenwich time is all over the universe. But my consciousness is not all over the universe, if that means that I am equally conscious of all the universe at once ; when I look out of the window, I see only Wetherlam, not Mont Blanc or the satellites of Sirius. There may be, and doubtless is, a sense in which the mind rises above the limitations of space ; but that is not to say that space is irrelevant to the mind.

It would appear, in fact, that things can only be distinguished when they are in some way homogeneous. We can distinguish two things of the same class or type without difficulty : we can point out that the difference lies in the fact that one weighs a pound and the other two pounds, or that one is red and the other blue. Differentiating things implies comparing them : and if we are to compare things they must be comparable. If two things have no point of contact, they are not comparable, and therefore, paradoxical as it may seem, they cannot be distinguished. Now in our original definitions of mind and matter, there was no such community, no point of contact. Each was defined as having unique properties of its own, quite different in kind from the properties of the other : and if this is really so, to compare and distinguish them becomes impossible.

But in practice the dualistic view is more lenient than this. It is not at all uncommon to hear mind described as if it were a kind of matter ; for instance, as a very subtle or refined matter : and it is equally common to hear matter spoken of as if it had that self-consciousness and power of volition which are characteristic of mind. These are dismissed as confusions of thought, mythological and unscientific ; but even if they cannot be defended they may be used as illustrations of the difficulty which mankind finds in keeping the ideas of matter and mind really separated. Once grant that mind is a kind of matter, and it becomes for the first time possible to distinguish them ; you have only to say what kind of matter mind is.

But, strictly interpreted, it seems that we can hardly accept the dualistic view whether as a metaphysic or as a hypothesis of science. It seems more hopeful to examine the other alternatives, materialism and idealism.

2. Materialism has been for many centuries, if not the most popular of all philosophies, at least among the most popular. Its popularity in all ages seems to be due very largely to the simplicity of the theory which it offers. Simplicity and clearness, the conspicuous characteristics of most materialistic theories, are very

high merits in a philosophy, and no view which is not simple and clear is likely to be true ; but the search after these qualities may easily lead to the false simplicity of abstraction and the false clearness of arbitrary dogma.

The most familiar criticism of materialism is that which points out its failure to account for certain facts in the world, and demonstrates the inadequacy of all materialistic explanations of such things as thought, action, æsthetic and moral values.   Such a criticism emphasises not the fact that no materialistic explanation of these things has ever yet proved satisfactory ; for that would be a superficial and unfair method of attack, seeing that no theory can claim to account for everything ; but rather the fact—for it does seem to be a fact—that the very method and presuppositions of materialism prevent it from ever coming any nearer to an adequate description of these things.   To take one case only, that of action : the peculiarity of action is that it is free and self-creative, not determined by any external circumstance ; but according to the materialistic presupposition, action must be a kind of motion in matter, and therefore, like all other motion, cannot be free and must be causally determined by external circumstances.   This is not to explain action, but to deny its existence.   And therefore materialism seems to be an instance of the opposite error to dualism ; the error of denying the existence of a fact because it will not fit into a system.   But it must not be forgotten that this error too is half a virtue ; and the respect with which philosophers such as Hegel treat materialism is due to the recognition that the materialist has the courage of his convictions and faith in his logic.

We shall not develop this criticism at length.   It has been often and brilliantly done by abler hands. We shall confine our attention to certain difficulties which arise not from the deficiencies of materialism in its relation to the facts of life, but from its own internal obscurities. The theory itself, in its simplest terms, seems to consist of two assertions : first, that all existence is composed of a substance called matter, and secondly, that all change is due to and controlled by a principle known as causation. The simplicity and. clearness of the theory, therefore, depend upon the simplicity and clearness of these two conceptions, matter and causation ; and we shall try to find out whether they are really as simple and as clear as they appear to be.

(*a*) Materialism offers us a philosophy, an explanation of the real world. It aims at showing the underlying unity of things by demonstrating that everything alike is derived from the one ultimate matter ; that everything is one form or another of this same universal principle. Now to explain a thing by reference to a principle implies that the principle itself is clear and needs no explanation : or at least that it needs so little explanation that it is more readily comprehensible than the things which it is called in to explain. If it were no more comprehensible than these, it would not serve to explain them, and the explanation would take us no further.

At first sight, matter does seem to be perfectly simple and easy to conceive. If it is regarded as a homogeneous substance, always divisible into portions which, however small, are still matter—divisible, that is, in imagination, even if not physically separable—we can no doubt imagine such a thing, and its simplicity makes it very well fitted to serve as a metaphysical first principle. And this conception of matter was certainly held at one time by physicists. According to the ancient atomic theory, matter was in this sense homogeneous and infinitely divisible, in thought if not in fact ; that is to say, you could not actually cut an atom in half, but it had halves, and each half was still a piece of matter. But this is not, I believe, held by scientists at the present time. The whole subject of the composition or structure of matter is one of extreme difficulty ; but if, for the sake of argument, we accept the view most widely held, we shall be compelled to say that matter is not, so far as we know, homogeneous, but is differentiated into a large number of distinct elements ; that these elements do seem to be made of the same stuff, that is to say, they are all composed of similar electrons arranged in groups of different types ; but that the way in which these different arrangements give rise to the different characteristics of the elements is a profound mystery. Further, the electron does not seem to be itself a minute mass of matter, like the old-fashioned atom ; it has none of the properties of matter, which are produced only (if I understand the theory rightly) by the collocation of electrons. Thus matter is a complex of parts which are not in themselves material. If we are pressed to describe these smallest parts, we shall perhaps have to say that they consist of energy. At any rate, they do not consist of matter.

The tendency of modern physics, then, if a layman's reading of it is to be trusted, seems to lie in the direction of abandoning matter as a first principle and substituting energy. This at least may be said without fear of contradiction : that matter is for physics not a self-evident principle of supreme simplicity, but something itself highly complex and as yet very imperfectly understood.

The simplicity of matter as conceived by ordinary materialism seems to be merely the simplicity of ignorance. Matter was supposed to be the simplest and least puzzling thing in the universe at a time when physics was in its infancy, when the real problems that surround the nature and composition of matter had not yet arisen. To-day, as Mr. Balfour says in a characteristic epigram, we know too much about matter to be materialists.

(*b*) But though the composition or structure of matter is thus too obscure a problem to serve as a support for materialism—so that even if everything is made of matter we are, metaphysically or in the search for comprehension, no further advanced, since we cannot say what matter is—it may still seem that the *operation* of matter is comprehensible and clear. The behaviour proper to matter is that controlled by causality; its motions are due not to its own spontaneous initiation but to external compulsive causes. Matter, if we cannot define it by its structure, can at least be defined as the field in which efficient causes are operative, in which we find the nexus of cause and effect universally maintained. We must turn therefore to this conception of causality, to see how far it will serve as an ultimate principle of explanation.

(i.) Causation is not merely a general principle of connexion between events; it is particular, not general, concrete, not abstract. That is to say, it does not simply account for the fact of change, but for the fact that this particular change is what takes place. One of the objections brought by the Renaissance scientists against the "final causes" or teleological explanations of Aristotelian science was that they supplied only general explanations, and gave no reason why the particular fact should be what it is; whereas according to the conception of efficient causes each particular fact has its own particular cause, and there is a definite reason why every single thing should be exactly what it is.

If we search for the particular cause of a given particular effect, we shall find this cause to be invariably complex, even when it is often described as simple. Thus, the gale last night blew down a tree in the garden. But it would not have done so except for many other circumstances. We must take into account the strength of the tree's roots, its own weight, the direction of the wind, and so on. If some one asks, "why did the tree fall?" we cannot give as the right and sufficient answer, "because of the wind." We

might equally well give a whole series of other answers:
" because the wind was in the north-west " ; " because
the tree had its leaves on " ; " because I had not
propped it " ; and so on. Each of these answers is a
real answer to the question, but none of them is the
only answer or the most right answer. No one of them
can claim to give the cause in a sense in which the
others do not give the cause. Is there then, we may
ask, such a thing as *the* cause at all? is there not simply
a number of causes? No, there does seem to be one
cause and no more ; but that cause is not one simple
event but a large, indeed an infinitely large, number
of events and conditions all converging to the one
result.

If we really wish to know the whole truth when we
ask for the cause of an event, then, it seems that we
shall have to enumerate all the conditions present in
the world at the time ; for we cannot assume any of
them to be irrelevant. The only real cause seems to
be a total state of the universe.

Further, if the whole present state of the universe
causes the fall of the tree, it also for the same reason
causes everything else that happens at the same time.
That is to say, the cause of the fall of my tree is also
the cause of an earthquake in Japan and a fine day in
British Columbia. But if one and the same cause
accounts for all these things, we can no longer suppose
that one particular event or set of events causes another
particular event, as such. Just as the only true cause
is a total state of the universe, so the only true effect
is a total state of the universe. To say that this gale
causes this tree to fall is doubly inadequate ; we should
say that the total state of the universe of which this
gale is a part causes the total state of which the fall
of this tree is a part. The nature of the connexion
between the gale and the fall of the tree in particular
has receded into impenetrable mystery. The only sense
in which causation explains the fall of the tree is that

we accept that event as part of the effect-complex and the gale as part of the cause-complex ; though why this should be so is quite unintelligible.

(ii.) Instead of many chains of cause and effect running as it were parallel, there is now only one such chain. But here again a very difficult problem arises. We generally think of the cause as preceding the effect; the chain is a temporal chain, spread out over time. Indeed, this is the only possible way of regarding the matter ; for if we regarded the cause as simultaneous with the effect, since each is a total state of the universe, each must be the same state ; and therefore the cause and the effect are not two different things but absolutely identical, and the law of causation would merely mean that the state of the universe at any given moment is what it is because it is what it is.

To avoid such a tautology we must define the cause as preceding the effect. This certainly involves difficulties; for of the causes we could enumerate, not all are events, and therefore it does not seem that they could precede the effect. The weight of the tree, for instance, does not in the ordinary sense of the word precede its fall. We speak of permanent causes, meaning such things as gravitation, which are never conceived as events.

But if we dismiss these difficulties and regard the cause as an event preceding the effect, we are equally far from explaining the effect. Admitting it to be comprehensible how the total state A causes the total state B, and B, C, we have merely explained C as the effect of A ; and this is only an explanation if we understand, and do not need an explanation of, A. And yet if C is a total state of the universe and A is another such state, why should one need an explanation and the other not ? We have, it seems, avoided the absurdity of tautology at the expense of falling into the equal absurdity of infinite regress. It is important, though at first sight not easy, to realise that this is an equal absurdity. There is a tendency to which we are all subject, to imagine that by deferring a problem we have made some progress towards solving it ; that if we are asked what made C, it is more scientific to answer "B made C, and A made B, but I don't know what made A," than to reply, "It made itself." One answer may be true, and the other false : but if we are in search of an explanation, there is no *a priori* superiority in either. Possibly the latter is slightly preferable, as it is better to give up a question one cannot answer than to answer it with an empty phrase.

(iii.) The view of causation as successive, then, does not seem really superior to that which regards it as simultaneous. The latter interpretation would make C its own cause, which contradicts the very definition of causality ; the former makes it the effect of something equally unexplained. That is to say, the causal view of the universe only accounts for the present state of things if it is allowed to take for granted, without explanation, the state of things in the past. Allow it to assume the universe as a going concern, and it can deduce you its successive states. The assumption is no doubt enormous ; but, after all, a theory is judged not by what it assumes but by what it does with its assumptions ; and if materialism really shows the connexion between different successive states of the universe, it has good reason to be proud of its achievement. But on closer inspection it appears that this result is only attained by means inconsistent with the materialistic assumptions.

Whether causation be regarded as simultaneous or as successive, the ultimate result is the same. The universe considered as a whole—whether a simultaneous or a successive whole—is conceived as causing its own states. There is in fact one supreme cause, which is the cause of everything, namely, the total universe. Now on the principles of materialism, on the principle,

that is to say, that everything is caused by something
else, we must go on to ask what causes the universe.
Plainly nothing can do this; for there is nothing outside the universe to cause it.   It seems, then, that in
order to make any progress at all, materialism has to
conceive the universe as an exception to its own fundamental laws.   The first law of matter is that it cannot
originate states in itself.   But the universe as a whole,
if it has any states, must originate them itself; and yet
if it does so it breaks the first law of matter; for it is
itself a material thing.   But the universe only means
all that exists; so if the universe is an exception to the
law of causation, everything is an exception to it, and
it never holds good at all.

It is hardly possible to avoid the conclusion that
materialism only succeeds as far as it does by implicitly
abandoning its own principles.   If it were rigidly held
down to the axiom that everything must be accounted
for by reference to something else, it could never make
headway.   As it is, it tacitly assumes that self-creation,
self-determination, is real and omnipresent; and this
assumption underlies all its progress.

(c) The materialist is not unconscious of this difficulty; he tries to evade it by pointing out that the series
of causes is infinite, and that therefore the problem of
ultimate causation does not arise; because there is no
such thing as " the universe as a whole."   This argument does not really remove the difficulty.   There are
certainly very famous and very difficult problems involved in the conception of an infinite series whether
of causes and effects or of anything else.   And it is
true that these problems are not solved by breaking the
series and interpolating a " first cause."   That would be
simply to lose patience with the problem and to upset
the chess-board.   But if I understand the argument,
its purport is that we cannot really ever supply an
explanation at all; that we have presented to our gaze
a mere fragment of a reality which stretches away into

darkness on either side of it ; the fragment being in itself, in the isolated condition in which we know it, necessarily incomprehensible because depending for its meaning on data which are concealed from us.

This sceptical turn to an argument which has, till now, erred rather on the side of confidence in its own simplicity need not greatly surprise us ; but it would perhaps be ungracious to acclaim it as marking the conscious bankruptcy of materialism and to pass on without further thought. It is doubtless true that all our knowledge is partial, and that unless we to some degree know everything we do not know anything fully. This is a difficulty which no theory can entirely avoid, and no theory, perhaps, can entirely solve. But in spite of its universality, it is, I cannot help thinking, more fatal to materialism than to other theories. Materialism presents us with a whole formed by the mere addition of parts which remain absolutely external to one another : and if this is so, it certainly seems that the infinite whole is unknowable, never really attained and therefore really non-existent. And the incomprehensibility or non-existence of the whole destroys the intelligibility and reality of the parts. If, on the other hand, it is possible to conceive a whole which is somehow not a mere sum of an infinite number of parts, but implicit in each single part while each part is implied in the rest, then such a whole would be knowable in spite of this sceptical argument ; for to the dilemma " either know the whole or do not pretend to know even this one part " we could reply that the knowledge of this single part is already knowledge of the whole. If we ask the time-honoured question, " How is knowledge possible ? " we can, I think, reply that if the universe were as the materialist depicts it, an infinite whole of finite parts in endless series, then knowledge of it would be impossible ; and that if the universe is to be knowable at all, it must be a different kind of whole, one of which we could say that each part by itself was already in some sense the whole. But a whole of this kind cannot be a merely material body.

3. It seems that the term matter is highly ambiguous. In one sense, it means merely something objective, something real, something which one handles or thinks about or uses, as we speak of the subject-matter of a book or the raw material of an industry ; these things may be either "material" or "spiritual." Secondly, it means the reality studied by physics in particular ; the chemical elements and their structure and relations. Thirdly, it means a homogeneous, inert and passive substance, whose changes are mechanically caused.

In the first sense, a colloquial rather than a philosophical sense, matter means merely reality. It is not opposed to mind ; mind is one class of it. Everything is matter in this sense.

In the second sense, the scientific sense, matter is equally real and perhaps equally universal. The third sense alone is philosophical ; and in this sense it would appear that matter does not exist at all. If, therefore, we deny the existence of matter, it must not be supposed that we wish to deny the reality of this chair and this table ; nor yet that we are casting doubt on the truth of physics. The view to which we seem to be led is that these things exist, but are not in the philosophical sense material ; that is to say, they are not composed of that homogeneous matter whose existence has been disproved by physics, and their behaviour is not dictated by the mechanical causation which we have criticised.

(*a*) This last point may create difficulty. It may be said that the whole work of the scientist consists of determining causes ; how then can we maintain that there are no causes, and not imply that his work is valueless ?

But it seems to be very doubtful whether science is really the search for causes, or even whether scientists themselves so conceive it. They would, perhaps, say that they were more concerned with the "how" of things than with their "why" : that they would be satisfied with accurately describing observed sequences, and rather suspect than welcome attempts to explain the underlying causes. Such attempts smack not of true scientific method but of the "occult qualities" of an unscientific age. In a word, science is the study of behaviour, the behaviour of men, plants, animals, or metals : and in no case need it advance any hypothesis as to why the behaviour of a certain thing should be what it is. It is difficult, perhaps impossible, to avoid framing such hypotheses ; but the hypothesis itself is not science but philosophy. Modern science is generally associated in practice with a materialistic philosophy ; but there is nothing in physics incompatible with the hypothesis that the complex of behaviour which the physicist calls matter is the outcome of a will or society of wills ; that the personality which directs our own bodily movements is present to some degree in each material atom, and that every event in the universe is willed.

It cannot be denied that at the present time scientists are very reluctant to accept such a hypothesis. It may be (they say) that some such view is widely held among philosophers ; or, at least, that few philosophers will accept a plain and sensible materialism. So much the worse for the philosophers. —The position is a curious one, and perhaps worth brief consideration. The scientist does not regard the philosopher as an expert in his own line, whose opinion on a metaphysical point can be accepted without question, just as an astronomer's would be accepted by a chemist. He regards philosophy as a subject on which he is entitled to an opinion of his own : and he expresses that opinion with perfect confidence, in defiance of the expert.

Such an attitude is really rather gratifying to the philosopher, who is always maintaining that philosophy is everybody's interest, and not the private preserve of academic specialists. Most philosophers, however, are ungrateful enough to turn a deaf ear to the scientist's overtures, and recommend him to mind his own business. But the scientist genuinely regards philosophy as vital to his own science ; though he may not use the word, which he tends to reserve as a term of opprobrium for other people's philosophy. More especially, he seems to regard materialism as the very foundation of his methods. Now if this were so, science would be in a highly precarious position ; for its methods would be founded on a theory which criticism has long ago discredited. For that materialism is discredited no student of philosophy can doubt.

On the other hand, materialism would never have arisen at all, unless it had to some extent satisfied the need for a theory. It may be wrong, but no theory is wrong from end to end. And this particular theory does rightly emphasise certain truths which are of great importance to the scientist. If it is asserted that all events are due to free volition, the scientist will very likely object to such a view because it seems to destroy the order and regularity of the universe. Make everything a matter of free choice, he would say, and you get chaos. Now this is not really true. A free will is not inherently chaotic ; to suppose that it is so is to confuse freedom with caprice and the absence of compulsion for the absence of rationality. But it is true that a free will may lapse into chaos, and that freedom may degenerate into caprice. A science, then, which is concerned primarily with regularities and generalisations depends for its very existence on the fact that the object it studies does not exhibit caprice : and this fact might be expressed by saying, " these things may be free, and act in this way because they choose to, but they act as uniformly and regularly as if they could not help it."

Science, however, does not remain permanently in

this stage of observing uniformities only. In its higher developments it comes to deal less with the general and more with the particular ; less with abstract classes and more with concrete individuals. This does not force it to abandon the hypothesis of mechanical causation ; for such a hypothesis is quite compatible with recognising that every individual is unique and must react in a unique way to the causes which move it. And in this uniqueness different individuals may still show resemblances. All this is true whether the changes that take place are willed or caused ; for as mechanism does not exclude uniqueness, so liberty is not incompatible with resemblance. The recognition that this is so removes the most reasonable and deeply rooted of all the prejudices in favour of materialism.

(*b*) Another merit of materialism is its insistence on fact, on reality as something beyond the power of the individual mind to create or alter. Matter is supremely objective. And when it is said that mind is the only reality, the suggestion at once arises that the world is less solid, less satisfying, less " real " than we believed. Not that we do not think of mind as real ; the plain man knows that his sorrows are mental, but does not think them any the less real for that. But he feels that to call his boots mental would be ridiculous. Some things, he supposes, are states of mind, and others not. And the attempt to define a non-mental thing (or " thing " *par excellence*) as a state of mind can only lead to the conception of something like it which is a state of mind—namely, the " mental picture " or imagination of a boot.

This consequence, the dissolution of the objective world into mere images or illusions, is one of the dangers against which materialism is very properly concerned to protest. But we have already argued that the distinction between two categories of reality, mind and matter, is no real help. And the danger against which the protest is made may perhaps be removed or diminished by pointing out that a confusion is implied between two senses in which we commonly use the word " thinking." In the first place, we use the word of real knowing, actual consciousness of some real thing ; in the second, of imagination, fancy, dreaming, or the mere play of opinion as opposed to knowledge. Now the imaginary boot belongs to the category of thinking only in the second, the inferior, sense of the word ; it is not thought at all as the term is used in philosophy. The " real " boot alone is in this sense fully worthy of the name thought ; it is the embodiment of the bootmaker's mind ; the " imaginary " boot is not a thought, only a fancy. What is wrong with it is not that it is only mental, but that, so to speak, it is not mental enough ; just as a cheap and superficial argument fails not because it is mere logic, but because it is not logical enough.

In the case of human products, indeed, we get nearer to their reality, not further away, by describing them as mental. A boot is more adequately described in terms of mind—by saying who made it and what he made it for—than in terms of matter. And in the case of all realities alike, it seems that the materialistic insistence on their objectivity is too strong ; for it is not true that we are unable to alter or create facts, or even that we cannot affect the course of purely " inanimate " nature. Materialism, in short, is right as against those theories which make the world an illusion or a dream of my own individual mind ; but while it is right to insist on objectivity, it goes too far in describing the objective world not only as something different from, and incapable of being created or destroyed by, my own mind, but as something different and aloof from mind in general.

(c) It appears, then, that we cannot conceive matter without ascribing to it some qualities of mind, nor mind without ascribing to it some qualities of matter. Matter cannot be subject to the law of causation, because that law itself, if our analysis can be trusted, breaks down under examination. Causation is pure passivity, and therefore cannot exist except relatively to some activity. If matter exists, mind must exist too. But we cannot conceive them as existing side by side ; we have already tried and failed to do so. We must think of matter as active as well as passive, and mind as passive as well as active. In one sense, then, everything is mind, for everything has in some degree the consciousness and volition which we described as mental. In another sense everything is material : for the real world does show that orderliness and objectivity for which materialism is fighting. But can we say that everything is matter with the same confidence with which we can say that everything is mind ?

Only if we bear in mind the ambiguity of the word. We distinguished three senses. In the first, the colloquial sense, all is certainly matter, for all is real and the possible object of knowledge. In the second or scientific sense, it may be true that everything is ultimately resolvable into the chemical elements, and that nothing exists except the matter of physics ; but we cannot (I think) assert this at the present stage of our knowledge. To ask whether mind is a form of matter or matter a form of mind is very largely a question of words. The important thing is that we should be able to bring the two into relation at all; that we should hold such a conception of matter as does not prevent us from admitting truth, morality, and life as a whole to be real facts, and that we should hold such a conception of mind as does not reduce the world to an illusion and experience to a dream.

The first of these errors is that of crude materialism, and the second that of an equally crude idealism. The view for which we are contending would claim the title of idealism rather than materialism, but only because the current conception of mind seems a more adequate description of the world than the current conception of matter. We are laying stress on the fact that the world is the place of freedom and consciousness, not of blind determinism ; and at present this can best be conveyed by saying that mind is the one reality. On the other hand, we do not wish to exclude, and should indeed warmly welcome, a higher materialism which could proceed on the understanding that the world while fully material was a conscious will or society of wills, and that its changes were not caused but chosen. Such a view would place matter neither above mind nor below it, would make it neither the eternal background nor the transitory instrument of spirit. It would regard matter as nothing else than mind itself in its concrete existence, and mind as the life and operation of matter.

The realisation of this higher materialism must wait till physics has advanced to a fuller conception of the nature of matter. No one, of course, can claim to possess now the knowledge which that fuller conception would bring ; but it may be possible to discern the direction in which progress is likely to come, and this we have attempted to do. The principle that all matter is in its degree a form of life seems to be continually suggesting itself as the solution of many problems in modern science, and appears in the most varied forms ; underlying both the assertion that nothing exists but matter and the counter-assertion that reality as we know it is not material at all.

CHAPTER III

We found in the last chapter that the issue lay less between materialism and idealism, in the sense of theories describing the world as matter and mind respectively, than between the passivity which we found to be falsely associated with the idea of nature, and the conscious freedom of mind. The former we found unsatisfactory as an account of the world, whether regarded from the side of science or that of philosophy; physics, as well as metaphysics, seeming only possible if the notion of blind causality were abandoned.

But if the universe is a whole of consciousness, of activity, of something that is at least better described as mind than as matter, in what relation does each part of it stand to the other parts and the whole? Is every part an independent and entirely individual mind (or piece of matter, if we prefer to call it so), or is there only one mind, of which every separate thing in the universe is a fragment and no more?

These two alternatives are generally known as pluralism and monism respectively. A thorough-going pluralism is intended to preserve at all costs the freedom and reality of the individual : but it does not tell us in what relation the individual stands to other individuals ; indeed, it does not tell us what in the first place constitutes individuality. For if the human being is an individual, what of the atoms of which his body is composed, or the many acts which make up the history of his mind ? Are they not individuals also ? And if so, how can he be at once a single individual and a group of individuals ?

It is equally easy for a thorough-going monism to assert the reality of the whole at the expense of the parts ; to deprive the human being of all true freedom and self-existence, and to reduce him to the position of a mere incident in the life of the universe. Of these extreme theories neither is satisfactory; and in the present chapter we shall attempt to reach a less one-sided view of the nature of personality.

What constitutes the self-identity of a person? What is it that makes him one ? And what, on the other hand, is the bond which makes a society one ? Are these two bonds at bottom the same ; that is, can a mind be at the same time one person and many persons, or is the self-identity of a person one thing and that of a society something totally different ?

1. In order to answer these questions we shall not inquire into the abstract meaning of the word personality. Many people maintain that personality, in its very meaning, implies limitation, finitude, imperfection, distinction from other persons, and the like ; and to make or to reject such assumptions at the outset would be to beg the question which we wish to answer. We shall begin by examining the relations which subsist between different persons as we know them, in the hope of thereby throwing some light on the nature of personality itself ; and these relations are the facts which we describe, on the side of thought, as communication, and on the side of will, as co-operation. For this purpose we can define a personality as this, if nothing more : the unity of a single consciousness ; while a society might be defined as the unity of different and co-operating consciousnesses. These definitions are only provisional ; but more than this we cannot say at the present stage of the inquiry.

(*a*) The fact of communication seems to be that two

H

or more persons can actually share the same knowledge. The condition is not satisfied by supposing that the one has a piece of knowledge merely resembling, however closely, the knowledge possessed by the other ; the two pieces of knowledge must be the same. There is a theory of knowledge which maintains that what I know is always peculiar to my mind, an " idea," as it is sometimes called, not an " object " ; a state of my own consciousness, not an independently existing thing. If this were the case, no two people could have the *same* knowledge, any more than two objects can have the *same* weight ; their weights might be equal, but the weight of each would be its own weight and not the other's. One thing cannot communicate its weight to another ; but one mind can, as we believe, communicate its thoughts to another. If this belief is true, knowledge is not a state or attribute of my mind in the sense in which weight is an attribute of objects.

But is the belief really true ? Is there such a thing as this communication at all ? Is it not rather the case that no two people ever quite understand one another, or ever see eye to eye ? Do not the facts rather favour the view that every one is sealed up in a world of his own ideas from which there is no egress and no channel of communication into the mind of any one else ? There is much truth in these contentions ; and we may grant —at least for the sake of argument—that no two people ever quite understand one another, that A never thinks in exactly the same way as B. But is the inference just, that communication is impossible ? We may not succeed in conveying our deepest thoughts to each other, but we continue to try ; and if the thing were an axiomatic and self-evident impossibility, how shall we account for the continuance of the attempt ? After all, a theory of knowledge must accept the fact of knowledge as a starting-point ; and it cannot be denied that partial, if not complete, communication is a fact. Nor can it be argued that this partial communication, which is all we can attain, is satisfied by the theory that my knowledge may resemble yours without being identical with it.   For however incomplete our communication may be, we have before us the ideal of complete communication; and the very imperfection of our attainment, our consciousness of its imperfection, proves that this ideal is really our constant aim.

We are justified, then, in dismissing these sceptical objections with the remark that, if they were true, they would falsify not only all else but themselves ; for the sceptic cannot seriously believe his own contentions so long as he tries to communicate his scepticism to us.

The unity of an individual was defined as the unity of a single consciousness.   But if two people are conscious of the same object, have they not thereby the same consciousness ?   We may be answered, no ; because there is more in any act of knowing than the mere object.   The knowing mind (says the objector) does not, so to speak, lose itself in the thing it contemplates.   If it did, then there would be no difference between my mind and yours so far as we were conscious of the same thing ; but as it is, knowing is a relation between two things, the subject and the object, the knowing mind and the thing known.   To forget the object makes communication impossible ; but to forget the subject makes all knowledge impossible.

This objection brings up one of the most difficult problems in philosophy, and one which it may seem both indiscreet to raise and presumptuous even to attempt to answer in brief.   But the attempt must be made, if we cannot hope to give a very satisfactory solution. To say that the mind is one thing and the object another is doubtless true ; but we cannot rest content with the statement.   It is true also that the relation between them is unique, and that attempts to describe it by analogy with other relations must always be as misleading as they have been in the past.   But it does not follow that, because it cannot be described by analogy, therefore it cannot be described at all ; still less that because it is unique therefore it cannot be understood.

Even to say that the mind is one thing and the object another may mislead. The mind is specifically that which knows the object ; and to call it a "thing" already suggests conceiving it as an object one of whose qualities is that it knows other objects—as this table is an object one of whose qualities is that it holds my paper—or, still worse, as a machine which turns out a kind of work called thinking, as a typewriter or a dynamo turns out its own peculiar product. The mind seems to be not so much that which thinks as the thinking itself ; it is not an active thing so much as an activity. Its *esse* is *cogitare*.

Again, just as the mind is not a self-identical thing persisting whether or no it performs its functions, but rather is those functions ; so the consciousness in which it consists is not an abstract power of thought which may be turned to this object or that, as the current from a dynamo may be put to various uses. All consciousness is the consciousness of something definite, the thought of this thing or of that thing ; there is no thought in general but only particular thoughts about particular things. The *esse* of mind is not *cogitare* simply, but *de hac re cogitare*.

I hardly think that any one will deny all this ; but it may still be said that though A's mind is nothing but his consciousness of *x*, and B's mind nothing but his, yet A's mind and B's remain absolutely different and individual ; since, though the object is the same and each admittedly knows the object, A's thought of it is distinct from the object itself and therefore from B's thought of the same object. It has already been admitted that each knows the same thing, but it is now argued that each knows it by having a "thought about it" which is peculiar to himself. I suspect this distinction between the object and the thought about it to be an instance of the confusion noted in the last chapter between thinking in the sense of knowing and thinking in the sense of imagining. My imagination of a table is certainly a different thing from the table itself, and to identify the two would be to mistake fancy for fact ; but my knowledge of the table, my thought of it in that sense, is simply the table as known to me, as much of the table's nature as I have discovered. In this sense, my "thought about" the table—what I think the table to be—only differs from the table itself if and in so far as I am ignorant of the table's real nature. My thought of the table is certainly not something "like" the table ; it is the table as I know it. Similarly, your thought of the table is what you know of the table, the table as known to you ; and if we both have real knowledge of the table, it seems to follow that our thoughts are the same, not merely similar ; and further, if the mind is its thoughts, we seem to have, for this moment at least, actually one mind ; we share between us that unity of consciousness which was said to be the mark of the individual.[1]

If it is said that the mark of the individual is not so much consciousness of an object as self-consciousness, and that each person's self-consciousness is unique, this is in one way, I think, true. It is true in the sense that in all knowing I am conscious of myself as knowing, and also in the sense that I am aware of my own history as an active and conscious being. But I am not aware simply of my own awareness in general, but

---

[1] I believe that the argument I have tried to express contains little if anything which contradicts the principles of either Realism or Idealism in their more satisfactory forms. There is an idealism with which I feel little sympathy, and there is a so-called realism which seems to me only distinguishable from that idealism by its attempt to evade its own necessary conclusions. But I do not wish to appear as a combatant in the battle between what I believe to be the better forms of the theories. Indeed, if they are to be judged by such works as Joachim's *Nature of Truth* on the one hand and Prichard's *Kant's Theory of Knowledge* and Carritt's *Theory of Beauty* on the other, I hope I have said nothing with which both sides would not to some extent agree ; though I can hardly expect to avoid offending one or other—or both—by the way in which I put it.

The reader who has not studied the latter works should be warned that the "New Realism" criticised in, *e.g.*, Professor Watson's *Philosophical Basis of Religion*, pp. 113-135, has no connexion with the realism which they defend.

of this object as a thing I am thinking about ; I may know that I am thinking, but not that I am thinking in the abstract ; only that I am thinking about this thing. Self-consciousness is not in this sense, so far as I can see, distinguishable from consciousness of reality in general. In the other sense, self-consciousness being taken as knowledge of myself as a historical person, this knowledge is by no means confined to myself ; others may in this sense know me better than I know myself.

Another possible objection depends on distinguishing two elements in knowledge, or two senses in the word knowing. There is, first, knowledge in the sense of what I know, the object ; and secondly, there is the activity of knowing, the effort which is involved as much in knowing as in anything else. Knowledge as a possession—the things we know—may be common to different minds, but, it may be said, knowledge in the sense of the activity of knowing is peculiar to the individual mind. It may perhaps be replied that since knowledge is admittedly an activity, an effort of the will, there is no difference between thinking and willing to think. And if two minds are identical in thinking the same thing, they are equally and for the same reason identical in willing to think the same thing. All knowing is the act of knowing, and therefore whatever is true of thinking *sans phrase* is true of the act or volition of thinking.

But the objection leads on to the second part of our subject. To distinguish thought as the consciousness of an object from thought as an act of the will is to appeal, as basis for the absolute plurality between persons, from the conception of knowledge to that of action ; and with this point we must proceed to deal.

(*b*) Every person, like every other fact in the world, is unique and has its own contribution to make to the whole ; a contribution which cannot be made by any other. This need not be emphasised, and certainly cannot be questioned. It is as true of the intellect as of the will; and yet we found that the statement "my knowledge is my knowledge" must not be so interpreted as to exclude the complementary statement that my knowledge may also be yours. This fact, the fact of communication, led us to the conclusion that if and when knowledge became in this way common property, the minds concerned became the same mind. But if two people can by communication share their knowledge, it seems equally certain that they may by co-operation share their aims and volitions. My actions are my actions; but yet they are not exclusively mine.

Just as our intellectual life consists very largely of the acquisition of knowledge from one person and the passing it on, when we have added what we can, to others, so our active life consists very largely of working at ideals which are the common property, if not of all mankind, at least of our particular society. Man does not struggle with either his intellectual or his moral problems in solitude. He receives each alike from his environment, and in solving them he is doing other people's work as well as his own.

Now if there is in this sense co-operation of wills, if two or more wills are bent on the same object, what is the consequence?

A will is not, any more than an intellect, an engine which produces certain results. We are sometimes tempted to think of the will as a central power-installation somewhere in the depths of our personality, which can be connected up with a pump or a saw or any other machine we may desire to use. In this sense we distinguish the will from the faculties, the one as the motive power and the other as the machine which it operates. But the will is not simply crude energy, indifferently applicable to this end or to that. Will is not only the power of doing work but the power of choosing what work to do. It is not in need of another faculty to direct and apply its energy. Will is, in short, always the will to do this or that : it is always particular, never merely general. The distinction between the will and the things which it does is a quite abstract distinction, like that between human nature and men. Human nature simply means the various kinds of men ; and my will is nothing more nor less than the things I do.

We seem therefore to be led to the same conclusion here as in the case of thought. If two people will the same thing, the personal distinction between them has given way to an identity, in virtue of which the two can be described as one mind.

2. It may be asked, if this identity were ever really established would it not be in fact self-destructive ? If the distinction between the two persons was absolutely cancelled, of what elements would the unity be composed ? For a unity that is composed of no elements at all cannot be anything. Not only does it like Saturn devour its own children but like the Kilkenny cats it devours itself. In short, the stress laid on the completeness of the unity is fatal to the theory ; for it turns the communion of different minds into a mere blank identity which is indistinguishable from a blank nothingness.

There are, I think, two answers to this question. We have already admitted elsewhere that every whole must be a whole of parts, and that all identity must therefore be an identity of differences. But if we look for the differences in this identity, they appear in two different ways, one from the side of the subject and one from that of the object.

(a) It must not be forgotten that the unity we have described is a unity of minds. Its very existence depends on the harmony between the minds ; and if by means of the unity one mind ceased to exist, the possibility of the union would vanish with it. For this reason the identity of wills does not result in a Spinozistic determinism of the one substance ; for the identity *consists in the fact that each wills the same thing* ; it is an identity not existing as a fixed unchangeable fact but *depending for its existence on the continued harmony of the two persons.* It does not unite them in spite of themselves, but because they choose to be united.

—Then the distinction is not absolutely cancelled, if the parties are free to dissolve it ; and if so, they retain their exclusive individuality all the time.—This looks unanswerable at first sight ; but I think that it is really a quibble. The argument involved is, that if a mind or society is capable of becoming something, that proves that it really is that something all the time. This seems to me to imply principles and consequences which I cannot accept. Because a good man may some day forget himself and commit a crime, that proves (says the argument) that he was not really good at all : it shows that he had in him the germ of the crime. Undoubtedly he had, if by the germ is meant the freedom of will which makes crime possible ; but to describe that as a germ of crime is most misleading, since the same thing is equally the germ of virtue. If by " germ " is meant any more than this—if it means a tendency which irresistibly grows into crime—then one must boldly reply that minds are not made like that ; what they do, they do not in virtue of irresistible " tendencies " but because they choose to do it.

So we should admit that because of its freedom a mind may forfeit the unity, whether with itself or another, to which it has attained. But that does not mean that it never attained it. For all the conquests of mind are made and held by its own freedom, held no longer than it has the strength to hold them ; and it can only lose this strength by its own self-betrayal.

(*b*) The identity also includes differences from the side of the object. If the object of the two minds was an abstract, undifferentiated one, then the two minds would also be a blank unity without difference. But this is not the case, for such an undifferentiated

unity nowhere exists.   In a sense, no two people ever
do, or ever could, think or will exactly the same thing.
This is not because unity is impossible ; it is not
because under the conditions of this imperfect world
we can never get more than an approximation to it.
If an ideal were not fully attainable by us here and now
it would not be a valid ideal for us here and now.
There is never an obligation to achieve the impossible.

Any truth or ideal of conduct expresses itself under
infinitely various aspects.   A single truth never means
quite the same thing to different minds ; each person
invests it with an emphasis, an application, peculiar to
himself.   This does not mean that it is not the same
truth ; the difference does not destroy the identity any
more than identity destroys difference.   It is only in
the identity that the differences arise.

The same is true of conduct.   My own duties are
the duties dictated by my situation ; no one else is
in precisely my situation and therefore no one else can
have the same duties.   And for the same reason no one
else can have exactly my desires.   But there is a community of aims ; and this community is not the barren
transmission of unchanging ideals, good or bad, in
which social life is sometimes thought to consist, nor
yet the equally abstract identity of the categorical
imperative, which only applies to everybody and every
situation because it abstracts from all the intricacies of real
life.   The community of aims consists in the fact that
what I want is something which I cannot have except
with your help and that of every one else.   The object
of my desire is one part of a whole which can only
exist if the other parts exist : or, if that way of putting
it is preferred, I desire the existence of a whole to
which I can only contribute one among many parts.
The other parts must be contributed by other people ;
and therefore in willing my part I will theirs also.

3. The unity whose possibility we are concerned
to prove is the fully concrete identification, by their

own free activity, of two or more personalities. This is not a universal condition, but an ideal ; it is the goal, not the starting-point, of human endeavour. But every real advance is like the spiral tunnel of an Alpine railway ; it ends, if not where it began, at least immediately above it. The end is not the antithesis of the beginning, but the same thing raised to a higher power. The end is a unity, and the beginning is also a unity ; but they are not the same unity. There is one perfectly concrete identity which consists in the highest degree of co-operation and the freest interchange of activities, and is destroyed when these fail : and there is another, an abstract, irreducible and indefeasible identity or union which subsists between any two parts of the same whole, and must continue to subsist as long as they remain parts. The whole, in each case alike, may equally be a society or a single person. We cannot maintain that a person is simply a necessary, indefeasible unity of those things which constitute his character, while a society is entirely dependent for its unity on the positive and conscious co-operation of its members, failing which it is no longer a society at all. A person is undoubtedly himself, and can never help being himself, whatever he does ; but this merely abstract unity, this bare minimum of self-identity, is much less than what we usually call his character or personality. That is rather constituted by the definite and concrete system of his various activities or habits. When we say, " I know his character, I am sure he will do this and not that," we mean that there is this systematic relation[1] between the different things he does, so that we can argue from one of them to the others ; that the connexion between his various actions is not the purely abstract connexion that they happen all to have been done by the same person. If there were no more than this abstract

---

[1] Not deterministic, because dependent for its very existence, as we said above, on his will ; and therefore capable of being infringed by his will.

unity, we could not say that a man had any positive "character" at all. To say " he is not himself to-day " appears, if we hold to the purely abstract sense of " self," merely ridiculous ; but in the concrete sense of " self," the sense in which the self is conceived as a co-operating unity of purpose, it has a perfectly real meaning.

The same distinction applies to the unity of a society. In one sense, any kind of relation between two people produces a kind of social union and identification ; in another sense, only the right kind of relation unifies them, and a different relation would destroy the unity. In the first case, their union is what I call the purely abstract unity ; in the latter, it is the concrete unity that has to be maintained by positive and harmonious activity. We cannot therefore say that, of these two kinds of unity, one is the kind proper to a person, and the other the kind proper to a society ; for each alike may apply to either. But, having examined the nature of the concrete unity, it is necessary that we should also examine, and indeed demonstrate the existence of, this abstract unity.

(a) But is unity the same as identity ? There seems at first sight to be a very decided difference between saying that two things are part of the same whole, and saying that they are the same thing ; the parts of one thing seem to be themselves quite separate and self-existent things, possibly depending on each other, but each being what it is itself, and not the others ; while the whole is simply their sum.

We have already expressed doubts as to the strict truth of this conception. We said in the last chapter that if a whole was to be knowable, it must be of such a kind that the parts are not simply added in series to one another, but interconnected in such a way that we can somehow say that each part is the whole. In that case each part would also be in a sense the

others. At the time this may have seemed highly
fanciful, if not a counsel of despair. What right, it
will be asked, have we to lay down *a priori* what must
be the nature of reality merely on the ground that
if it is not thus, it is not knowable? How do we
know that reality is knowable? And even if we are
assured on that point, and legitimately assured, is it
not a monstrous inversion of the true order to argue
from knowability to reality?

I am not sure that it is. Knowledge is as much a
fact as any other; and if the business of a sound
theory is to account for the facts, a theory which does
not admit of the world's being completely known is,
to say the least of it, incomplete. The modern
impatience with such forms of argument may be
partly based on their connexion with false theories
of what knowability means, but it is certainly due in
part to the prejudice that the facts of the external
world are certain, while the nature of knowledge and
the processes of mind are unknown; so that to argue
to the nature of the real world from the nature of the
mind is arguing from the unknown to the known,
attempting to lay down by insecure deductions from
a discredited metaphysic things which could be easily
ascertained by appealing to the natural sciences. This
" positivistic " attitude is lamentably self-contradictory ;
for if we are not to believe in the full knowability of
the world, what becomes of the facts of science? And
if we are, why should we hush the matter up? We
cannot pretend ignorance of the nature of knowing
while we claim that science gives us real knowledge
and philosophy only a sham.

I think therefore that we need not retract the
argument. But as it stood it was incomplete ; for
it merely sketched the conditions of a satisfactory
view of the relation of the whole to its parts, without
explaining how they can be fulfilled.

Let us take as an instance any whole consisting of

three parts, x, y, z. It makes no difference whether it is a machine with three working parts, a society of three members, a stanza of three lines, or a syllogism containing three propositions. Each part has its own nature, its own individuality, which is in the strictest sense unique ; and apart from the contribution made by each several element the whole would not exist. Change one part, and the whole becomes a different whole. Not only does the whole change, but the apparently unchanged parts change too. Substitute, in a tragic stanza, a grotesque last word, and the opening lines become suddenly instinct with ridiculous possibilities. Substitute in the society a new third man, and not only is it now a different society but the social value and function of the unchanged members is altered.

On the other hand, the part that is removed is no longer what it was. A man may resign his place in a society because he feels that he is no longer what the society requires him to be ; and in that case his resignation gives him a new freedom. If he leaves it with no such reason, his personality is mutilated by the separation ; one side of his character is cut off and frustrated. The separation of the part from the whole destroys part and whole alike. The part survives only as something different from what it was ; it has to readjust itself, if it can, and become something else. If it cannot do this, it dies outright. The whole must in the same way readjust itself to the new conditions and become a different whole : otherwise it also dies.

It follows from this closeness of interconnexion between the whole and its parts that the question " what is x ? " cannot be answered merely by saying " x is x." X only exists as x in relation to y and z. If y or z were removed, x would no longer be what it was : it would have to become something else, or failing that, cease to exist at all. Consequently if we ask for a definition or description of x the only true reply is to describe it in its full relations with y and z. That is to say, a definition of x can only take the form of a definition of the whole system xyz. To explain the nature of the part we have to explain the nature of the whole ; there seems to be no distinction between the part and the whole, except that the part is the whole under one particular aspect, seen as it were from one point of view. In the same way and in the same sense y and z are identical each with the whole and with each other and x. Each part is the whole, and each part is all the other parts.

A distinction is sometimes drawn which avoids this conclusion. There is, we are told, a difference between what a thing is in itself and what it is in relation to its context or to the whole of which it is a part. X as a thing in itself remains (it is said) the same : it is only its relations with other things that change, and these are merely external, and do not affect its real nature. It is true that nothing is really destroyed by depriving it of its context. But this is only because we cannot deprive it of all context. A lintel taken out of its place in a house and laid on the ground has a context, though not an architectural context ; and Robinson Crusoe in his solitude has a perfectly definite environment, though not a human environment. However much we try to remove all context from a thing, we can do no more than to invest the thing with a different context. Indeed, there is a sense in which we may still call the stone a lintel and Robinson Crusoe the member of a human society ; for the history of a thing in the past and its capabilities for the future are as real as its present situation, though in a different way. The isolated stone lying on the ground may still be called a lintel ; but this is so only on account of the house from which it came (strictly, it *is* a stone that *was* a lintel), or into which it will be built (it is a stone that *will be* a lintel), or even because of the imaginary house which we can, so to speak, construct round it now (it is a stone that *might be* a lintel).

The character or self of a thing, what it is, cannot be distinguished from its relations. Architecturally, the stone *is* a lintel ; that is its own character. But this character only consists in the fact that it stands in a certain relation to other stones which together with it make up the doorway. Geologically, the description of the stone is identical with the description of its place in the geological series. Every characteristic of the thing turns out to consist in a relation in which it stands to something else ; and similarly, if we began at the other end we should find that every relation consists in a quality of the thing itself. This double movement is only not a vicious circle because, of the two things which thus turn into one another, each is already identical with the other.

The inner nature of the part x, then, is entirely constituted by its relations to y and z. And therefore x is simply one way of looking at the whole xyz ; and y and z are other aspects of the same whole. The part is not added to other parts in order to make the whole: it is already in itself the whole, and the whole has other parts only in the sense that it can be looked at from other points of view, seen in other aspects. But in each aspect the whole is entirely present.

If we take the case of a musical duet, we have a whole which is analysable into two parts. At first sight, we might be tempted to describe the relation between them in some such way as this : there are two separate things, two musical compositions, one called the treble and the other the bass. Each is an independent reality, has a tune of its own, and can be played separately. On the other hand, they are so arranged that they can also be played both at once ; and when this happens, they produce an æsthetic value greater than either can produce by itself. The whole is the sum of its parts; and the parts in combination remain exactly what they were before.

This description seems at first sight reasonable; and it is familiar as underlying, for instance, the Wagnerian view of opera. If you take two arts and add them together—so that view runs—you produce a new art twice as great as either.

But is the æsthetic value of a duet really equal to the sum of the values of its parts played separately? No such thing. The query of one instrument may indeed be in itself a beautiful phrase, independently of the answer given by the other; but as seen in relation to that answer it acquires a totally different emphasis, a meaning which we never suspected. The accompaniment part, or even the solo part, played by itself, is simply not the same thing that it is when played in its proper relation to the other. It is this relation between the two that constitutes the duet. The performers are not doing two different things, which combine as if by magic to make a harmonious whole; they are co-operating to produce one and the same thing, a thing not in any sense divisible into parts; for the " thing " itself is only a relation, an interchange, a *balance between* the elements which at first we mistook for its parts. The notes played by the piano are not the same notes as those played by the violin; and if the duet was a merely physical fact, we could divide it into these two elements. But the duet is an æsthetic, not a physical whole. It consists not of atmospheric disturbances, which could be divided, but of a harmony between sounds, and a harmony cannot be divided into the sounds between which it subsists.

The same is true of any really organic whole. A scene of Shakspere can be regarded as so much " words, words, words," and, when so regarded, it can be divided into what Hamlet says and what Polonius says. But the real scene is not mere words; it is the interplay of two characters. It is one thing, not two. To subdivide it would be not to halve but to destroy its value. Even a baby can be cut in two, if it is regarded as a mere piece of flesh ; but the resulting portions would be the halves not of a baby but of a corpse.

A unity of this kind exists not only in harmonious and fully co-operative wholes, but equally in everything that can be called a whole at all. Whatever the particular relation in which x stands to y and z, it is still true that each part is but an aspect of the whole and identical with the other parts. X, y, and z may be parties to a quarrel ; but they are in that case just as much parts of the same whole, just as closely identified with one another, as if they were allies in a common cause. This kind of identity, therefore, is to be sharply distinguished from the contingent unity, the unity of co-operation, which we described at the beginning of this chapter. Upon this distinction turns the whole argument of this and the succeeding chapters.

(*b*) The universal and necessary identity, the abstract identity of mere co-existence, is often taken as supplying the key to all the difficulties with which the religious or philosophical mind feels itself beset when it deals with the problem of personality. All personalities are components of a whole, the universe ; and therefore, by the above argument, they are all necessarily identified with each other and the whole, that is, with the universe considered as homogeneous with them, an absolute mind, God. The line of thought seems to be simple and impossible to refute : and if this is really so, it establishes at a blow the existence of God and his perfect immanence in humanity, and leaves nothing more to be achieved or desired.

To reject such an argument altogether would certainly be a mistake. It is true that, whether we like it or not, whether we live up to our position or deny our responsibilities, we are so intimately connected with each other and the divine mind that no act concerns the doer alone. This assumption is fundamental. But the error lies in mistaking this fundamental assumption for the final conclusion ; in assuming that this elementary, abstract unity is the only one which concerns us. In point of fact, it concerns us, if at all, certainly in the very lowest possible degree. In practical matters, a constant which is always present and can never be altered is best ignored ; and indeed this purely abstract identity is so shadowy a thing that it is hard to see what else to do. To call this formless and empty abstraction "the Absolute" is merely to abuse language; and to suppose that this is all philosophy has to offer in place of the concrete God of religion is completely to misunderstand the nature and aim of philosophy. There have been and no doubt still are people who claim the title of philosophers on the ground that they habitually amuse themselves with abstractions of this kind. But it is a pity that their claims have been and still are taken seriously.

The Absolute, as that word is used by any philosophy worthy of the name, is not a label for the bare residuum, blank existence, which is left when all discrepancies have been ignored and all irregularities planed away. An arbitrary smoothing-down of the world's wrinkled crust is not philosophy, but the vice against which all philosophy wages an unceasing war. A real philosophy builds its Absolute (for every philosophy has an Absolute) out of the differences of the world as it finds them, dealing individually with all contradictions and preserving every detail that can lend character to the whole.

Here as elsewhere the instinct of religion is the deliberate procedure of philosophy at its best. When religion demands a personal God, a God who has a definite character of his own and can, as the phrase goes, take sides in the battles of the world, it is really asserting the necessity for this concrete characterised Absolute, as against a sham " philosophy," the philosophy of abstractions, which assures it that since God is all, he cannot have any one attribute rather than its opposite ; that since he is infinite, he cannot be a person ; that since he is the strength of both sides, the slayer and the slain, he cannot himself fight on either side.   In the Absolute, we are told, all contradictions are resolved, and therefore all distinctions vanish ; good and evil are no more, for that of which each is a manifestation cannot itself be either.   A personal God, creating the world and sustaining it by the might of his will, is a mythological fiction.   A God who is in any sense transcendent and not purely immanent is inconceivable, and even imaginable only to the half-savage mind which anthropomorphises everything it does not immediately understand.

So " philosophy " browbeats common sense till the latter for very shame yields the point ; tries to recast its religion, if it still ventures to have one, on lines of pure immanence, and if it cannot make the immanent God seem as real and vivid as the transcendent, humbly puts the failure down to its own philosophical short-comings.   For "philosophy" has assured it that Reality, properly faced and understood, will more than console it for its lost fairyland.   There is little ground for surprise if after such experiences religion hates and despises the very name of philosophy.   The formless and empty Absolute of this abstract metaphysic perished long ago in the fire of Hegel's sarcasm ; and it is curious to find the very same pseudo-Absolute, the " night in which all cows are black," still regarded as being for good or evil the essence of philosophical thought.

(c) It is time to leave these abstractions and turn to the other kind of identity, the concrete identity of activity.   A mind is self-identical in this sense if it thinks and wills the same things constantly ; it is identical with another, if it thinks and wills the same things as that other.   This might seem to imply that in the first case there was no possibility of change or process within the limits of the self-identity ; and in the second case that the personal distinction between the two minds was reduced to a mere illusion. But, (i.) so far is it from being true that a thing to be self-identical must not change, the very fact of change proves its continued identity; for only a thing which is still itself can be said to have changed. This however is abstract identity only, and it might be imagined that concrete identity was not compatible with change. But this is a mistake. It is the property of truth to present itself under the aspect of innumerable differences ; and yet within these differences it is still one. If we reflect upon some particular fact, we can see it take under our eyes a hundred different forms, emphases, shades of meaning. In following out this process, it does in a quite concrete sense change ; and the thinking of this change is a real mental process, in the only sense in which any thought can bear that name. (ii.) The identity of two minds which think the same thing does, as we have already seen, in one sense abolish the difference between them ; but this very abolition is only possible through the free and independent activity of each separate mind. Difference is not simply absent ; it is overcome.

Now these two cases are typical first of the self-identity of God, and secondly of his identity with the human mind. God is not a mere abstract unity ; he is a mind, and as such he can possess the higher unity of self-consistency. This attribute must necessarily belong to him if we are right in regarding him as omniscient and perfectly good. An omniscient mind is one whose beliefs are never false, and whose field of knowledge is not limited by any ignorance. This is the only type of mind which can be described as entirely consistent with itself. Any false belief, introduced into a system of judgments otherwise true, must breed contradiction; for its implications cannot be developed to infinity without coming into conflict with some other belief. Again, any limitation, any gap in one's knowledge, may have the same result; for different truths often seem to conflict until new knowledge explains them both and shows them to be harmonious. But two truths can never in reality contradict one another, and therefore a mind which believed all truths would have within itself no contradiction at all.

In the same way, we can conceive a mind which willed, not indeed all the actions, but all the good actions in existence. Of the different actions in the world, some are in antagonism to others, and therefore it is impossible for a mind to will both except at the cost of losing its concrete unity, its own positive nature, and becoming a formless something indistinguishable from nothing. A mind which willed all the good in existence would display this concrete unity to the full; for two duties, two good things, can no more conflict than two true things.

Each of these conflicts does often seem to take place. Two statements which contradict each other do very often seem to be, each from its own point of view and within its own limitations, true. And two people who are supporting opposed causes may seem to be both in the right. But in the former case we know that the conflict is only apparent; that if each disputant understood the other, it would in so far as each is right disappear. And similarly in the other case, though the fact is not such a universally recognised axiom in ethics as the " law of contradiction " is in logic, it is true that of the two opponents one, or possibly both, must be in the wrong; or, if that is not the case, the opposition between them must be illusory. Good is self-consistent just as truth is; and just as a mind which believes all truth is supremely self-consistent and self-identical, so it is with a mind which wills all good.

Further, this divine mind will become one with all other minds so far as they share its thought and volition; so far, that is, as they know any truth or will any good. And this unity between the two is not the merely abstract identity of co-existence, but the concrete identity of co-operation. The abstract unity would remain even in the case of a mind which (if that be possible) knew nothing true and did nothing right. There is a sense in which whether we will it or not we are indissolubly, by our very existence, one with God ; that bond it is not in our power to break. But the highest and most real identity with him we can only possess in the knowledge of truth and the pursuit of goodness.

Thus God is at once immanent and transcendent ; and man can be regarded as, on the one hand, a part of the universal divine spirit, and on the other, as a person separate from God and capable of opposition to him. God is immanent because all human knowledge and goodness are the very indwelling of his spirit in the mind of man ; transcendent because, whether or not man attains to these things, God has attained to them ; his being does not depend upon the success of human endeavour.

Such a mind as this, omniscient and perfectly good, is conceivable ; but the conception may be called a mere hypothesis. I think it is more than this. Every good man, and every seeker after truth, is really, even if unconsciously, co-operating with every other in the ideal of a complete science or a perfect world ; and if co-operating, then identified with the other and with an all-embracing purpose of perfection. There really is such a purpose, which lives in the lives of all good men wherever they are found, and unifies them all into a life of its own. This is God immanent ; and it is no mere hypothesis. Is it equally certain that he also exists as transcendent, or does that remain a hypothesis, incapable of proof ? Is God only existent as a spirit in our hearts, or is he also a real person with a life of his own, whether we know him or not ?

The difficulty of answering this question is bound up with a well-known philosophical puzzle, the puzzle of how to prove the existence of anything except as present to the mind. If it is true that things cease to exist when we are not thinking of them, and that the people whom we generally suppose to be real independently of our dealings with them exist only as and when we are conscious of them, then it follows by the same argument that God is immanent only, and exists nowhere but in the minds of men. But we cannot really believe that these things are so. And to suppose that the spirit of goodness of which we are conscious in our hearts has its being there and there alone is no less fantastic than to suppose that the friends with whom we converse are only the projection upon nothingness of our own imagination. The arguments for pure immanence are at bottom identical with the philosophical creed of subjective idealism, and with that creed they stand or fall.

This conception of God as perfectly wise and good avoids at least the faults of an indefinite and empty abstraction. But is it any more than the other horn of an inevitable dilemma? God, as we have conceived his nature, is good indeed, but not omnipotent; wise, but unable entirely to control the world which he knows. He is the totality of truth and goodness, the Absolute of all the good there is; but the world's evil remains outside this totality, recalcitrant to the power of God and superior to his jurisdiction.

Here, it is sometimes said, lies the parting of the ways between religion and philosophy. Religion must at all costs have a God with a definite character of his own; philosophy must have an all-embracing totality, a rounded and complete universe. And when it is found that God, to be good, cannot be all, then religion and philosophy accept different horns of the dilemma, and from this point travel in different directions.

But such a solution really annihilates both philosophy and religion. The "universe" which philosophy is supposed to choose is again the empty abstraction of a something which is nothing definite; it is not an Absolute, but only the indication of an unsolved problem. And for religion too the problem is unsolved; for it refuses, and rightly refuses, to believe that a limited God is its last word. It cannot accept the antithesis between God and the world as final. Either it declares its faith in his ultimate omnipotence, in the final identification of the seemingly opposed terms, or it relapses into the pessimism of a forlorn hope which can do no more than hurl defiance at a world of evil which it cannot conquer. Of these alternatives, the highest religious faith unhesitatingly chooses the first, at the risk of being accused of a sentimental optimism. But the attitude so chosen is the only consistent one ; for the pessimist's defiance of the world already achieves in some degree that very victory which he pronounces impossible.

Each solution, then, the undefined Absolute and the limited God, is provisional only, a working hypothesis and no more. An undefined Absolute is not an Absolute, and a limited God is not a God. Each alike can only be made satisfactory by acquiring the character of the other ; and hence the problems of religion and philosophy are one and the same.

This brings us face to face with the question of evil. How can a world whose elements are at variance with one another be, except in a merely abstract sense, one world at all? How can the existence of a perfectly good God be reconciled with the reality of minds whose will is the very antithesis of his own ?

CHAPTER IV

EVIL

1. THE difficulty with which we have to deal is expressed by the simple religious mind in the form of the question, "Why does God, being good, allow the existence of evil in his world?" And, in the absence of any immediate answer, the solution is suggested with almost irresistible force that God, if omnipotent, cannot be really good. We have indicated in outline the conception of a God who united in himself all goodness; but the existence of evil seems to prove that if he exists he is no more than one among many limited minds, good so far as he goes but not able to expel all evil from the universe. If it persists in the refusal to exchange a real God for a colourless Absolute, religion seems forced to accept a God who is hardly more than another good man.

(*a*) We are apt to suppose that this is the nemesis of a peculiar weakness in religion. If it had adopted the more rigorous and thoughtful methods of philosophy, we imagine, it would have avoided these dilemmas and perplexities. It has committed itself to a mythological and fanciful procedure, half-way between thinking and dreaming, and this is the result. I think such an explanation is entirely superficial and untrue. The problem expressed above in religious language can be readily translated into terms of philosophy, and constitutes for philosophy as serious a difficulty as it does for religion. It may be roughly sketched from this point of view as follows:

If the world is will, it must be a will of some definite kind ; a good will, for instance, or a bad will. But things are done in the universe which fall under each of these classes. If one part is bad, how can we call the whole good, or *vice versa* ? We may try to evade the difficulty by replying that the world is not one will but many wills ; or (which comes to the same thing) a single will fluctuating between good and bad. This is no doubt true ; but is it a society of wills? and if so, why is its behaviour not social? Again, we may reply that it is not really will at all in the ordinary sense, but mere matter or a " blind will," which does not know what it is doing, or a "super-moral will," which does not care. But we cannot escape by taking refuge in materialism ; for a materialistic universe could never give rise to the conflicts of which we complain. A universe which was purely mechanical would be perfectly smooth and self-consistent in its behaviour ; for machines only "go wrong " relatively to the purpose of their makers. Nor do the other hypotheses improve matters ; for they do not explain how the conflicting elements came into existence. If the universe had a " blind will," it could not include in it my will which is not blind. If the Absolute were superior to moral distinctions, it would exclude instead of including the consciousness of a moral person.

And indeed a " blind will " is a contradiction in terms, for a will which did not know what it was doing would be not a will but an automaton, a mechanism. And a "super-moral Absolute " is, I think, a no less contradictory idea ; for it implies that the Absolute is something which does not explain but merely contradicts the things we know ; that reality is not richer or fuller than experience but simply different, so that experience is illusory and reality unknowable.

Philosophy has, no doubt, some answer for these questions. But so, within its own system of ideas, has religion. For each, the problem is one of extreme difficulty ; for neither is it literally insoluble. A philosophical problem cannot be insoluble, though it may be too hard for you or me to solve satisfactorily, and it may quite well be insoluble in terms of a certain theory which is so framed as to ignore or deny the facts on which the solution depends. But a theory which shows this kind of deficiency is, strictly speaking, incapable of solving not only that particular problem but all problems connected with it, that is to say, since all philosophical problems are interconnected, all problems whatever. A question is only unanswerable when the data for answering it are not in our possession ; for instance, we may ask in vain for historical information about a fact of which there are no records. But in philosophical questions the data are ready to our hand, and only require analysis and description. The same is true of theological problems. In the language of orthodoxy, God has revealed his nature to man, if man will receive the revelation ; in philosophical terms, the character of the perfect or ideal mind is implicit even in the imperfections of mind as we know it. We must assume then that the problem is soluble and see what we can do towards solving it.

(*b*) It is important to state as clearly as possible wherein the problem consists. I think we may distinguish three different questions, each of which may be asked about three different things ; and all these questions are liable to be presented simultaneously as the Problem of Evil. Ultimately, no doubt, they cannot be separated ; but it does not promote their solution if we fail to distinguish them at all. The three things are error, pain, and evil ; understanding always by evil the badness of a will. The three questions are, first, How is the thing to be defined or described ? second, How does it come to exist ? and third, What does it prove ? what can be the character of the whole of which it forms a part?

(i.) I think, though not without great hesitation, that the problem of pain in general is not the same as the problem of the other two forms of evil. When people speak of the " problem of pain," they seem generally to mean by it some question like this : " Why, if God is as you assert both omnipotent and benevolent, does he permit his creatures to suffer things which any kindly-disposed man would give his life to prevent? Either God allows these things, in which case he is less bene-volent than man, or else he, too, would like to stop them, in which case he is as impotent as ourselves."

Now it is not difficult to see that this question assumes as obvious a certain theory of God which may be described as purely transcendent theism. God is conceived as a ruler imposing his will on a passive creation by means of laws in whose effect he does not share. It seems to me that the sting of the problem entirely vanishes if the distinction between activity and passivity is removed ; if, in other words, we conceive God not as imposing his will on the world from without, but as himself sharing in all the experiences of other minds. Some such view as this we are now assum-ing as proved ; for the result of the last two chapters will not permit us to regard the creator as severed from his creation, or the whole as external to its parts.

It is sometimes said that all pain is due to an evil will, which inflicts it directly upon sufferers or, indirectly, upon the wrongdoer himself. All pain is thus either the natural consequence of sin, recoiling on the head of the sinner, or else the effect of his sin on others. If that were so, pain would be absent from a universe in which there was no evil, in the strict sense of that word ; and the problem of pain would be identified with the problem of the bad will.

This is a position which, as I suggested above, I do not feel able to accept. Evil wills are responsible for a vast proportion of existing pain : for much more, perhaps, than we generally imagine. And empirically, I suppose, the nearest approach to a painless life is to be found in the companionship of persons whose

attitude towards one another most nearly approaches
to perfect love and harmony. On the other hand—
empirically once more—the attainment of any fulness
and depth of experience seems to be necessarily painful
as well as pleasant, even for the noblest minds.
Æsthetic experiences like hearing music (or, again,
seeing a play finely acted) involve a kind of pain
which is very acute, and cannot be confused with the
pain of hearing bad music or music badly played.
There seems to be something of this nature—what we
might call a tragic element—in all the highest forms
of life. It does involve pain ; but it also involves
pleasure, which transfuses the pain while it does not
for a moment disguise its painfulness.

If this view of the matter is right, the practical
problem of pain is not how to avoid it but how to lift
it to a heroic level ; and the presence of pain in the
world is not a contradiction or an abatement of the
world's value and perfection. Pain may make the
world difficult to live in; but do we really want an
easier world ? And if we sometimes think we do, do
we not recognise that the wish is unworthy ?

At any rate, the wish is useless. I do not think it
serves any purpose to imagine hypothetical worlds in
which this or that element of the real would be absent.
And it does seem to me that pain is such an element.
Whether or no it is always due to our own imperfection
or sin or the sin or imperfection of others, it cannot
ever be eliminated, simply because a perfection of the
type required can surely never exist in a world of free
agents ; because even if no one did wrong, the effort
of doing right would still be difficult and painful just
so long as the practical problems offered by the world
were worth solving. Pain seems to involve imperfection
only in the sense in which any one who has a thing to
do and has not yet done it is imperfect ; and in that
sense imperfection is only another name for activity
and perfection for death.

(ii.) Error and evil are more difficult even than pain to assign, as they stand, to a place in the universe. It is sometimes taken as self-evident that a good world cannot contain pain. I have said that I think this assumption is mistaken. But I do think it is self-evident that a good universe cannot contain either evil or error just as they stand. This is the problem with which we shall deal in detail. The other two questions must be also raised : first, What are these things, and secondly, How do they arise ?

The latter question can be answered easily or not at all, according to its meaning. In one sense, the answer simply is, " Because people do them " ; that is to say, there is nothing to prevent any one from doing wrong or from making a mistake, and it depends on himself whether he does so or not. A man does right not only because it is God's will but because it is also his own will ; God could not make him do right if he did not want to. And therefore God cannot prevent his doing wrong. In another sense, the question implies a desire to go behind this freedom of the individual, and to discover why he chooses to do this and not that. But in this sense the question is meaningless ; for there is nothing behind the will which makes it do one thing rather than the other.

(iii.) The other question would seem at first sight easy. An error is defined as thinking something that is not true; and a bad action as doing something wrong. But we have defined thinking as the consciousness of a reality ; and therefore error is not thought, for if it were consciousness of reality it would not be error. But what can error be if it is not thought ? How can you make a mistake without thinking ? It might be ingeniously replied, when you make a mistake you are nor *really* thinking at all : you only think you are thinking. But alas ! we are no further ; for if all thinking is true, then in thinking that I thought I must really have thought. Nor is it any better to say that I imagined that I thought ; for if so the point is that I mistook, on this occasion, imagining for thinking. Nor can we say that I felt as if I had done a piece of thinking when really I had not ; granted that there is a peculiar flavour in real thinking, how does it come to be associated with something that is not thinking? and if it is liable to be so associated, why, knowing this, should I let it mislead me?

We cannot avoid the difficulty by defining error as an act not of the intellect but of the will : for instance, the arbitrary assertion of a thing which the evidence does not warrant. If this were so, there would be no difference at all between making a mistake and telling a lie. A man may be blamed for his mistakes, and a mistake may be described as a moral offence, perhaps with justice; but that does nothing to clear up its nature.

It may be replied, all this comes of committing yourself to a faulty theory of knowledge. First you propound a theory on which error cannot possibly exist, and then you are illogical enough to complain that you cannot understand error. It is a well-known fact that there are theories of knowledge of this sort ; yours is one of them ; and you had much better give it up.—I should be most willing to do so, if any other theory were more successful. But the critics who use the language I have just quoted have as a rule nothing better to offer in exchange than an empiricism which, while carefully designed to admit the possibility of error, omits to allow for the possibility of truth. Indeed a cynic might be tempted to divide theories of knowledge into those which admitted the possibility of truth but denied the existence of error, and those which admitted error but denied the existence of truth. Neither type of theory can be satisfactory ; but it may be argued that a theory which at least admits the existence of truth is likely to contain more of it than the one which does not. The only third alternative is the refusal to admit a theory of knowledge at all. And this too I cannot accept ; for we do talk about knowing, and our statements about it must mean something, and be either true or false.

The same difficulty arises in connexion with the definition of wrongdoing. To put the dilemma briefly, a person doing wrong must know that it is wrong ; for otherwise, though we may blame him for culpable negligence or obtuseness, we do not blame him in the full moral sense as deliberately guilty. And yet it would seem that the essence of doing wrong is to persuade oneself somehow that it is really right, or excusable, or not so very wrong. The fact seems to combine two contradictory attitudes—the doing a thing although you know it is wrong, and the thinking that it is right when it is not.

One is sometimes tempted to say that these things, evil and error, are really self-contradictory attitudes of mind, mental confusions ; and that therefore it is no use trying to have a clear theory of them, since the facts themselves are not clear. But is it so ? If a state of mind were self-contradictory, how could it exist ? If it is coherent enough to exist, why should it not be coherent enough to be described ? Superficial thought, we must repeat, finds no difficulty in describing them because it does so, naïvely, in self-contradictory terms ; it is only analysis of the terms used that reveals the difficulty.

Even if it is impossible to define them, need that hinder our inquiry? No one has ever defined goodness, for instance, and yet moral philosophy exists. The parallel is comforting, but I fear misleading. The famous difficulty in defining goodness does not exclude the possibility of conceiving goodness. We know perfectly well what it is, and the only sense in which it is indefinable is that, being unique, it cannot be described in terms of anything else. But I do not think the same is true of error and evil. The difficulty here seems to be not that we know what they are but cannot

K

give a formal definition of them, but rather that, though we recognise them when we see them—sometimes—we do not know what they are at all.

Having no answer to offer to such a fundamental question, would it not be best to put up the shutters and go home? Is it not mere trifling to offer theology the assistance of so impotent a metaphysic? The criticism is perfectly just. We cannot hope to solve, or even usefully to discuss, the problem of evil unless we know what evil is. But our real position is worse than the criticism suggests. It implies that there is a retreat open to us; that we can, and in fairness ought to, renounce our attempt to solve these problems rationally and take refuge in a decent agnosticism. This we cannot do; for it is not unequivocally true even that we are ignorant of the nature of evil. We do recognise it when we see it; and we can make some statements about it, or at least show that some accounts of its nature are false. The only escape from our situation is to build on these facts, however slight they may appear. An agnostic withdrawal from the argument would, by denying their existence, commit itself to a falsehood no less than the dogmatic denial of the difficulties.

This, then, must be our course. In the first place, we shall examine and criticise certain current conceptions of evil; secondly, we shall try to determine the relation of evil to good within the universe. Such a procedure, after the admission that we cannot define evil, is illogical, absurd, perhaps even dishonest; its only excuse is that the alternative is worse.

2. The theories of evil which I intend to criticise agree in treating evil as somehow illusory or non-existent. The universe, according to this type of view, is perfectly good, and everything is good just so far as it exists; evil is non-existence, deficiency, negativity, the past stage of a process, and so on. I shall treat these views in some detail because I believe that there

is a certain amount of truth in them, and that they fail in general through not successfully defining what they mean by real and unreal ; whereas their opposites, the pessimistic views, contain I think less truth and are sufficiently dealt with by the main argument in § 3.

It is perhaps worth remarking that optimism and pessimism alike create a spurious unity by denying one side of the contradiction ; each is a symptom of exactly the same fault. It is often said that optimism results from a sentimental temper which refuses to face facts ; and this is perfectly true. But it is equally true of pessimism. To deny the existence of facts simply because they are pleasant is no less sentimental than to deny their existence because they are unpleasant. It is one kind of sentimentality, and not an attractive kind, that refuses to see anything outside itself but one all-embracing *Weltschmerz*, and anything within but its own " spasms of helpless agony." [1]

It ought also to be said that in criticising views of this type I am not criticising those philosophers such as Plato, Spinoza, or Hegel, to whom they often owe the language in which they are expressed, if no more. I am rather criticising tendencies of popular thought which have a certain superficial resemblance to their philosophies.

(a) The simplest type of optimism is perhaps to be found in the not uncommon statement that evil does not exist at all; that there is no such thing. As stated, this is merely a paradox which has no meaning until it has been explained : and to explain it generally involves explaining it away. The only sense in which it is a serious theory is that it sometimes takes the form of asserting that no one ever really does wrong, and our beliefs to the contrary come from misinterpreting the actions of others, and indeed our own. That is to say, there is no evil ; there is only error, the erroneous belief that evil exists.

---

[1] W. James, *Varieties of Religious Experience*, p. 163.

While granting fully that a completer knowledge would explain as good many actions which we imagine to be bad, I cannot think this view plausible. Led by the difficulty of conceiving how a bad action can exist, it suggests that none do exist, and that the apparent cases to the contrary are really cases of false judgment. It can only advance this conclusion because it has never realised that exactly the same difficulty attaches to the conception of the false judgment. If the moralist had by chance been a logician instead, he would have raised the question how people make mistakes : and he might have answered that they do not ; they only tell lies. What appears to be an error, he might triumphantly say, is only a moral obliquity.

If this seems a far-fetched objection, it may be simply expressed thus. Evil does exist. People do wrong. There is no reasonable doubt on that point. But as soon as we begin thinking about it, we find it so difficult to understand that we are tempted to explain it by appeal to a parallel difficulty, that of error. The two are, I think, parallel ; but neither throws much light on the other because each is equally obscure. And if we deny the existence of the one, the same difficulties when we faced them would compel us to deny the existence of the other.

(b) An argument closely resembling this admits that bad actions are done, and does not flatly say that we are mistaken in calling them bad ; but merely that in so doing we are expressing a limited point of view. From this finite point of view we are right, it is said, in calling them evil ; but from a wider point of view either they would be seen as good or perhaps the difference between good and bad would disappear.

We cannot, however, dispose of the distinction between right and wrong by saying that it is relative to particular points of view. The argument seems to confuse several different things ; and it is perhaps worth while to distinguish at least some of these.

(i.) " What is right for one society," we are told,
" is wrong for another. It would be sadly narrow-
minded to wish that every portion of the human race
could live under the same kind of social organisation.
On the contrary, to confer the blessings of civilisation
upon the savage often means nothing but to force
him into a mould for which he is quite unfitted and
in which he can never be either happy or prosperous.
His institutions are the best for him, and ours are
the best for us ; and when we ask what is the right
manner of life, the question always is, for whom?
Nothing is right in itself, in isolation from the
circumstances which make it right."

Much of this is perfectly true. Not only is one
people's life not good for another people, but even
one man's meat is another man's poison. Every race,
every person, every situation is unique, presents unique
problems and demands unique treatment. And if
the argument means no more than that we must not
impose the treatment proper to one case on another
(as we frequently do), it is legitimate. But those who
use it seem often to imply that, since every evil is
relative to some situation, a perfectly free man who
had no particular prejudices and no merely parochial
interests would be superior to the distinction between
good and bad. This of course is absurd ; for every
man must be an individual and stand in some definite
relation to other individuals ; and these relations will
determine what is—and really is—right and wrong
for him.

(ii.) The argument may also be taken to imply
that there is a specifically moral way of looking at
things, which is one out of a large number of possible
ways, and not the truest. We may approach actions
with the question on our lips, " are they right or
wrong ? " and in that attitude we shall understand
less of their real nature and value than if we asked,
" are they adequate, or fitting, or noble, or splendid ;

do they show a grasp of the situation, a penetrating intellect, a determined will, a subtle sense of beauty ? "

We do certainly feel a sense of irritation with people who insist upon raising the moral issue to the exclusion of all others. They seem to think that it only matters if a person had good intentions, and makes no difference whether he is a competent man or a muddler. It does make a difference ; and either goodness is only real goodness when united with competence, or else there are other things to value a man by besides his goodness.

But these other things do not outweigh goodness, still less make it disappear. Whatever other things there may be, there is morality ; but the argument seems to suggest that because there are other standards of value, therefore the moral standard cannot be maintained. If this is its meaning, it is no more than an attempt to distract attention from one question by raising others.

(iii.) Thirdly, it may mean that morality is a " category " of the human mind as such, which would be absent from a better or more highly-developed type of mind. It is a limitation, but a necessary limitation of humanity. We cannot deal fully with a contention of this kind without examining its presuppositions in a theory of knowledge derived more or less from Kant. But I think such an examination would bear out the plain man's feeling that an argument like this is not playing the game ; that it is not fair to tell him that the construction of his mind is such that he cannot help having convictions which nevertheless are not really true. The philosopher who tells him so seems to imagine himself as behind the scenes, privileged to criticise and correct the workings of the mind which after all is just as much his mind as the plain man's. If the conviction is inevitable, how is scepticism as to its truth possible ? The critic of the mind is doing something which looks very like playing fast and loose with his convictions.

(c) Another appeal to ignorance is contained in the view that evil is justified by becoming a means to good. This argument is reinforced by the parallel of pain. The dentist inflicts pain ; but he only does so to save us from a much greater amount of pain in the future. Our condemnation of the evil in the world is thus explained as the rebellion of ignorance against the surgery of an all-wise Creator.

As applied to pain, the argument is not without great value. But even so, it should be observed that the pain of dentistry remains pain, and is not made pleasant by the fact that it absolves us from future pain. And the really skilful dentist can almost, if not entirely, banish pain by means of anæsthetics. Is God less skilful ?

In point of fact the parallel does not apply to evil at all. The evil consequences of an evil act might well be so thwarted by circumstance or overridden by omnipotence that they never affected the person whom they were, perhaps, intended to harm. But the moral evil of the act lies not in its success but in the intention, and no overruling can affect the intention or make it less evil. A bad action may be providentially a means to good ; but that does not destroy the agent's badness of will. The problem of moral evil remains untouched.

(d) Another common account of evil appeals to the logical conception of negation, asserting that evil though real is merely negative. I do not think that this does much to clear it up. If two things are conceived as opposites, either indifferently may be described as the negation of the other ; but neither is, so to speak, inherently negative. The distinction between affirmative and negative is a distinction of words, not of things. A " negative " reality would be quite as positive as an " affirmative " reality. I imagine that this theory really means that good is normal or natural or something of the sort, while evil is abnormal and only exists as an exception, and could never by itself make a world. This idea seems to me to be sound, and we shall meet it again ; but I do not think that it is well expressed by saying that evil is merely negative.

(e) The last theory we shall examine defines evil by reference to the conception of evolution. Our sins, according to this theory, are the habits proper to a past stage in the evolutionary process, lingering on like rudimentary organs into our present life. Here again there is a fact at the bottom of the theory. It is true that the particular way in which we go wrong is often explicable by reference to past habits of which we have never entirely got rid. But the question still remains unanswered why we should go wrong at all. Nor is the theory fully true even so far as it goes ; for atavism is not a crime, and just so far as our " crimes " are really cases of atavism they are not culpable ; unless indeed it is supposed that our evolution is entirely in our own hands. But if that is so, morality must be called in to account for evolution, not *vice versa.*

It is a striking fact that the biological conception of evolution has never yet produced anything but confusion when applied to philosophical questions. The reason seems to be that it gives, in the form in which it is commonly held, no answer to the one question with which philosophy is concerned. As we said in a former chapter, science (including the theory of evolution) is simply a description of behaviour, and advances no hypothesis as to why things behave as they do. The theory of evolution is a purely historical statement about the way in which life has developed ; ethics is concerned with the force of will which lies behind all merely descriptive history. It makes little difference to the scientist whether he regards evolution as a purely mechanical process or as directed by the volition of conscious agents ; but until this question is answered, evolution is simply irrelevant to ethics.

In this case, for instance, there are three conceivable hypotheses, either of which might be adopted by science without greatly altering its particular problems; but for ethics they are poles asunder. (i.) If the process is really mechanical, the habits may be explained, but they are not sins. (ii.) If a central mind such as that of God directs the process, then the habits in question are not our sins but God's. (iii.) If, as above suggested, the process is in the hands of the evolving species, the bad or superseded habits are sinful, but they are not explained. Thus the evolutionary view of the question only restates the problem in terms which conceal the fact that no solution is offered.

3. We can now proceed to the last and for our purpose the most important question, namely, how evil and error can coexist in the same universe side by side with truth and goodness, and how a universe so composed can be described; whether, that is, we can call it either good or evil. The answer to this question can only be reached by drawing out the implications of two statements : (i.) that the universe contains good and evil side by side ; (ii.) that everything in the universe stands in some relation to everything else.

(a) Suppose I intend to write a complete account of any subject concerning which there is in existence a considerable body of scientific information and opinion. There are, broadly speaking, two ways in which I can go to work. Either I can simply collect all the opinions, false and true, which have been held on the subject, and write them down side by side ; or else I can sift them out, correcting the false by the true, and presenting a body of statements which is, so far as I can make it so, absolutely true. These two methods typify two senses in which we can speak of a totality : first, a mere juxtaposition of conflicting details, and secondly, an organised and coherent whole. Which of these is in the truest sense a totality, and in which sense do we speak of the totality of the universe ?

The mere collection would be repugnant to the scientific mind.   It is the work, a critic would say, not of a thinker but of a sciolist ;   the book that quotes infinite contradictory authorities and " leaves the reader to choose between them " is not history, but the gratification of a jackdaw's collecting-mania.

It appears on examination that the scientist's prejudice is well founded.   The mere collection misrepresents the facts which it pretends to describe.   A's opinion took its form through the detection of an error in B's, and B's by refuting C's.   Simply to quote A, B and C side by side is precisely to miss the historical development and continuity on which all three depend.   The mere collection is not a totality ; it is a number of different things whose relation to one another is denied, an abstract plurality which is not a unity.   Unity can only be introduced into it in one way : by thinking out the relations of each opinion to the rest.   When this is done, as it is done by the true historian of thought, it is found that even where one opinion contradicts another there is the closest of relations between them ; that they are successive attempts to reach the truth on this subject, and that each statement sums up in itself the truth expressed by previous statements and is itself the starting-point for further research.   This way of putting it is not affected by the breaks and discontinuities which there must be in any tradition.   We are not arguing that there is a steady and continual progress towards truth, independent, as it were, of intellectual effort ; but that every truth takes its form by correcting some error, and that therefore in the totality of the science the error does not stand alongside the truth, but is corrected by it and disappears.   Consequently to the historian of thought these errors do not form part of the science at all.   He knows and records the fact that they have been made ; but as the science comes to him they have been eliminated by the thought which has supplied their correction.   (It is not implied that at any given point of history *all* the errors have been eliminated.)

In brief, truth and error cannot coexist in relation with one another. If they are brought into contact, the error is abolished by the truth. A truth and an error about one and the same subject can only exist so long as they are kept separate in water-tight compartments; that is, so long as the person who believes them both is unconscious, while believing one, that he also believes the other, or so long as the person who believes one does not come into contact with the person who believes the other.

Our problem was something of the following kind. God is conceived as omniscient; all his beliefs are true. But there are also many false beliefs in existence. These are *ex hypothesi* not shared by God. Therefore the totality of the universe, including as it does the false beliefs as well as the true, is more inclusive, larger, so to speak, than God who only includes the true ones. God therefore is not all-inclusive, not universal; he is only one among many minds. To a person who argued thus we might now answer, are you in earnest with the idea that the world is a totality? Do you believe that it is a society of spirits in communication with one another? If so, you are convicted out of your own mouth. For if the world is a totality it already shows the same perfection which is ascribed to God. The true opinions in it eliminate the false, leaving nothing but truth. And therefore the all-inclusive universe is not larger than, but identical with, the perfect God.

According to this conception the universe includes all error and yet it includes no error. Every error is a fact that happens in history, and so is part of the universe; but the false opinion in which the error consists disappears from the universe when faced with the truth which contradicts it.

Two objections at once suggest themselves. First, why should it be assumed that truth must drive out error?

Why should not error drive out truth? Certainly this may happen. But I do not think any one would believe that this is the way in which any science has actually progressed for long together. A mind which really grasps a truth is not shaken in its belief by denials, because it sees the point of view from which the denial proceeds and can formulate the truth so as to include that point of view. In doing this it would not become less true. But if error embarked on the process of including other points of view, even if these others were themselves erroneous, the error would gradually approach nearer to the truth, for to believe all the different errors about any subject may come very near to knowing the truth.

The second objection is this : Why assume that the universe is a unity at all? how do you know that its parts are all in some relation to each other? Indeed, are you not arguing in a circle by first assuming it to be a whole or system, and then arguing that it must on that account be systematic? It may be that we are wrong in assuming that there is one universe. But I do not think that it is a mere assumption. The alternative hypothesis would be that there are within it elements entirely out of relation to one another ; that is, in terms of our view, that there are minds which are concerned with objects so entirely disparate that they cannot either agree with or contradict one another. But in the nature of the case, if there are minds which have no characteristic and no object of thought in common with ours, we cannot possibly conceive them, far less prove or disprove their existence. And if we are right in thinking that our philosophy concerns the nature of mind as such, it must be a description, whether true or false, of any mind that exists.

In one sense, it is perhaps true to say that the universe is not a totality. Taken at any given moment, it is incomplete. There are still undissolved errors, unfinished thought-processes. The world we see around us is not a stationary, already-existing, "given" totality, but a totality in the making : its unity consists only in the striving towards unity on the part of the minds which constitute it. This does not mean that its completion lies at some point in the future ; it is a completion that never is and never will be attained for good and all, but one which is always being attained. The life of the world, like the life of a man, consists in perpetual activity.

(b) As the new knowledge supplied by true judgments eliminates from the mind and annihilates erroneous judgments, so, it would appear, a good motive arising in the will annihilates a bad. This conception is at first sight not so clear as the other. If I have acted upon a bad motive, how can I then entertain a good motive bearing on the same situation ? For I have already done the bad thing, and I cannot now do its good alternative. The bad act is a historical fact, and nothing can now change it. That is true, but the same is true of a false judgment. If I have made a mistake and published it, I cannot by discovering my error undo all the harm which my statement may have done. Nor can I even change the fact that I did believe it. The most I can do is to cease to believe it, and substitute a true belief. In the case of a wrong act this change of attitude is also possible. I may be what is known as a hardened sinner, that is to say I may refuse to admit that I was wrong to act as I did ; but I may also change my attitude towards my own conduct from one of self-approval or excuse to one of condemnation. The evil with which we are concerned is, as we said above (§ 2, c), not the consequence but the badness of the will itself ; and this can only be overcome in one way, by the turn of the will from evil to good. This attitude of a will which in virtue of its own goodness condemns an evil act is called, when the evil act is a past act of its own, repentance ; but it is essentially not different from the choosing of the good and rejection of the bad among two alternatives offered to the will as present possibilities. It is thus parallel to that judgment of the truth which either overthrows one's own past mistake, or avoids a mistake in the present.

The two cases seem to be parallel throughout. Just as one cannot believe at once the truth and the error, so one cannot at once embrace the bad and the good motive ; and just as the truth drives out the error, so the good motive expels the bad. If then we put once more the original problem, it will reappear in the following shape. God is the absolute good will: his will includes all good actions and nothing else. How then can we identify him with a universe which includes both good and bad ? The answer will be that within the same totality of will there cannot be both good and bad motives bearing on the same action or situation. Just so far as totality is attained, the good will must eliminate the bad, and therefore the universe conceived as a totality of will must be entirely good. Nor is this argument dependent on the hypothesis, if it is a hypothesis, of a perfectly good God ; for it follows from the conception of the universe as containing both good and evil, without any assumption except that the parts of the universe are in relation to one another.

Here again, however, there are two points which must be emphasised. The first is that we have not, by a dialectical juggle, swept evil out of existence or proved that the universe is perfect just as it stands, and considered at any given moment. The perfection of the universe depends on its being a totality ; and, as we have already said, it is only a totality *in posse*, not a totality *in esse*. The non-existence of evil, its destruction by goodness, is neither an accomplished fact nor an automatic and inevitable conclusion. It is a process, and yet not a process if that means something never actually fulfilled ; rather an activity, a process like that of seeing or thinking, which is complete at every moment and is not a sum of successive states. The triumph of good over evil is not a foregone conclusion but, as it were, a permanent miracle, held in position by the force of the good will.

The other point relates to the possibility of an advance in the other direction; of the elimination not of evil by good but of good by evil. Is it not possible for all good to disappear and for the universe to become entirely bad? It is certainly possible within limits for error to drive out truth and for vice to drive out virtue. A man may become worse and worse, and lapse into a quagmire of wickedness from which it is progressively harder to escape, just as he may become more and more deluded till he lapses into idiocy. But it would seem that his very delusions must be based on some lingering remnant of truth; that gone, there would be no more hallucination, for the mind would simply have vanished. A man who knew nothing at all could hardly be said to make mistakes. And so I think vice always exists in a will which is not only potentially but actually to some extent virtuous; that the impulses of which evil is made, the faculties which carry it into effect, are themselves virtues of a sort. It is often said, but I find it hard fully to believe it, that impulses and faculties are in themselves neither good nor bad, but indifferent: the mere material out of which goodness or badness is made. I may be wrong, but I cannot help feeling that the admiration with which we regard the skill, resource, and devotion of a great criminal is a partly moral admiration, and that the evil which fights against good is itself fighting in defence of a good. Can we call it a perverted good, or a right ideal wrongly followed? These may be meaningless phrases, but they seem to me to express something that is missed by the sharp dualistic distinction between good and evil.

It seems clearer that evil can only exist in an environment of good. No society is ever utterly depraved, and crime owes its existence to the fact that it is exceptional. The success of a fraud lies in the victim's being off his guard ; if he was expecting it and trying to do it himself it would not be a fraud, any more than to deceive an opponent at chess is a fraud. The same applies to crimes not obviously social ; they necessarily stand out against a background of normal life which is not criminal.   Good acts, on the other hand, do most emphatically not require a background of evil.

It seems then, if these arguments are justified, that there cannot be even a totally bad person, and *a fortiori* not a totally bad society or universe.   If coherence and totality are to be attained at all, they must be attained by complete goodness.   And, if we are right, they can be thus attained.   A will may be absolutely good ; not in the sense that it is ignorant of evil, but in the sense that it knows the evil and rejects it, just as a sound intellect is not ignorant of possible errors, but sees through them to the truth.   This state is equally perfection, whether it has been won through error and sin, or without them ; for the mind is not in bondage to its own past, but may use it as the means either of good or evil.

There is much concerning the manner in which evil is overcome by good that belongs to a later chapter ; but we can already give some kind of answer to the question with which we began.   We asked, why does God permit evil ?   He does not permit it.   His omnipotence is not restricted by it.   He conquers it. But there is only one way in which it can be conquered : not by the sinner's destruction, which would mean the triumph of evil over good, but by his repentance.

PART III

FROM METAPHYSICS TO THEOLOGY

L

CHAPTER I

In this third part we shall attempt to use the results of the foregoing chapters as an approach to some of the more technical problems of theology. We shall take what I suppose to be the central doctrine of the Christian faith, and ask what light is thrown upon it by the conclusions we have reached as to the relation between God, man, and the world on the one hand, and between good and evil on the other. By the central doctrine of Christianity I mean that taking-up of humanity into God which is called the Incarnation or the Atonement, according as the emphasis is laid on God's self-expression through humanity or man's redemption through the spirit of God.

It must be understood that I approach this subject from a single definite point of view. I shall make no attempt to state in detail the beliefs of the Church, or of any other body. Some initial statement is necessary, but this may be very brief and can perhaps be presented in a form to which no school of Christian thought would very strongly object. The details will then be developed by applying to these statements the general principles set forth in the second part. It follows that these chapters aim not at orthodoxy but at the faithful translation into theological terms of the philosophy already expressed in the preceding pages. I might, no doubt, have gone on to consider whether the ultimate theological results were in agreement with the beliefs of orthodox Christianity. But I have not done this; not through any indifference to the question, for it would be hypocritical to conceal my hope that the conclusions here advanced may really agree with the deepest interpretation of the Christian creed, but because the task involved in such a comparison would take me far beyond the limits of this volume.

1. The doctrine of the Incarnation, in its most central characteristics, may perhaps be outlined in some such way as this. There was a certain historical person who was both divine and human. He was truly and actually divine with the full characteristics of Godhead, and fully and completely human in all the individuality of manhood. He was not, however, a compound of two different personalities, but one single personality.

This statement of two natures in one person may be taken as our starting-point. It represents approximately the " formula of Chalcedon " ; and it must be noticed in passing that this formula is no more than a starting-point. As stated, it puts the problem without offering any solution at all. It is our task to discover how such a problem can be solved. The problem, more precisely, is not for us, " Was such and such a person both divine and human ? " but, " How is it possible for a person to be both ? " That is to say, we are setting aside all questions as to the " historical Jesus " and attending merely to the necessary implications of the doctrine. Our answer will be in the form, " if any man fulfilled such and such conditions, he was perfectly divine as well as perfectly human ; but it is not our purpose to inquire whether the conditions have been fulfilled."

(*a*) How can there be an identity between a human being and God ? There are two types of answer to this question. The first type runs thus : Man, simply as man, is already divine. Man is spirit, and God is spirit, and between the two there is no sharp line of demarcation. This truth, the divinity of man, the fatherhood of God, is the message of Jesus and the creed of Christendom.

The second type of answer lays stress not on the nature of mankind as a whole, but on the nature of the one man who alone is believed to have been truly and fully divine. He, and no other, has lived a perfect life ; he and no other has set before the world in his own person an example of love and power which it cannot choose but worship.

These two answers seem not only different, but utterly and radically hostile ; representative of points of view between which there can be no truce. The first is the purest immanent Pantheism, the second an absolutely transcendent Theism. If all men are equally divine by their very manhood, then the claim of one to be especially so is indefensible. The claim, then, must be explained away or boldly pronounced a mistake. Perhaps, it is sometimes suggested, "the divine man" means no more than "the man who first discovered the divinity of man." On the other hand, if one man alone is divine, it cannot for a moment be admitted that the same is true of all other men ; for that would be to sacrifice the whole value of the one unique life.

It is clear that if the first type of answer is adopted, the original question falls to the ground. We need no longer ask, how is it possible for a man to be divine ? because no man is anything else. But we are left with two difficulties. In the first place, can such a view be made to square with the words or the spirit of the New Testament narratives ? and secondly, is the view itself a sound and reasonable one ?

With the first difficulty we have nothing to do. We have to ask whether it is reasonable to hold that all men are divine in such a way that no one is more divine than any other. And here we may recall the two senses in which the word identity was found to be used. There is, it will be remembered, a purely abstract identity, an identity which cannot be diminished or

increased, which subsists merely in virtue of the continued existence, in whatever relation, of the things
identified.   There is also another identity, not abstract
but concrete, subsisting in virtue of an identity of
thought or purpose between the persons concerned, and
existing only so long as that identity is maintained.

Now in the first sense every man must be, so far as
he exists, identical with every other and with God.
There must be some relation between God and any man,
even a man ignorant of God or hostile to him.   And
where there is some relation there is some identity.
Not indeed a low degree or small amount of identity,
for identity only exists absolutely : it is either complete
or non-existent.   According to this kind of identity,
then, every man is already and fully divine, and it is
not possible that any one man should be more so than
any other.

But the other kind of identity depends not on bare
existence but on the kind of existence which a free being
chooses to have.   According to this kind of identity,
it is clear that any man who fully knew the mind of
God, and whose will was bent on the same ends as the
divine will, would be himself both man and God in one,
completely human and completely divine.   In this sense
not every man is divine ; indeed it is rather to be
doubted whether any man ever has been or ever could
be.   This question we shall raise later.

The position which we described as Pantheism, then,
namely that every man is necessarily and unchangeably
divine, is very far from being false ; but is equally far
from being the whole truth, and to represent it as the
whole truth is to make a serious mistake.   The divinity
of every man, simply as man, is no more than an abstract
divinity, the guarantee of a fuller and more concrete
union.   And this concrete union is only to be attained
in and by the identification of the self in all its aspects
with the perfect mind of God.

The kind of identity which we are to consider is the

latter kind only. Of the former, there is indeed nothing more to say; it is a pure abstraction, and of an abstraction we can say no more than that—in its own abstract way —it exists. The divinity for the possession of which we reverence the Founder of Christianity, the union with God which we ourselves desire to attain, is no abstraction ; it is a concrete and living activity, and therefore it depends on, or rather consists in, not the bare unchangeable nature of man as man, but the positive character of his life, his individual thoughts and actions.

God and man are identified in one person, concretely identified, that is identified not only fully but also in the highest possible sense, when a human being has an individuality of his own, identified with that of God in the unity of all his thought and action with the divine knowledge and the divine purpose. This ideal person, in whom Godhead and manhood not only coexist but coincide, I shall call the Christ ; but without, for the purposes of this chapter, assuming his identity with the Jesus of history, or indeed assuming that such a person has ever lived at all.

(b) It may be objected to such a conception, that the supposed union is impossible because no one man—no single individual — can comprehend completely the nature, and identify himself with the purpose, of God the absolute mind. The knowledge and manifestation of God are, it may be said, attained little by little, through an infinite process of historical growth and development. Not one man, but the whole of humanity is necessary to reveal God ; and not humanity only, since in any one class of facts God can only reveal as much of his nature as that kind of fact will express. A single man can only express one very limited side of the divine character, which is too large to be confined within the circle of a finite personality.

This objection carries great weight and seems very convincing ; and it has often led to the adoption of a view according to which the revelation in Jesus is only one of an infinite number of revelations, each and all contributing something to the total knowledge of the infinite God. And yet if God is infinite and each manifestation of him is finite, how can any number of manifestations come any nearer to expressing his full nature? A large number of units is no nearer infinity than a single one. Again, is it really justifiable to describe a human personality as finite at all? We saw reason to maintain in a former chapter that a mind was only definable in terms of the object of which it was conscious; and if God is infinite and man is really conscious of God, it seems to follow that man thereby becomes infinite. It is sometimes said that for this very reason man can never know God; but to lay down *a priori* what a given mind can and what it cannot know in virtue of its own constitution is to begin at the wrong end. The mind is what it makes itself; and its finitude or infinity (if the words mean anything) consists merely in its failure or success in the attainment of its desire.

The objection in fact is precisely an instance of the materialistic type of thought which we criticised in a former chapter. It represents God as a whole composed of separate and mutually-exclusive parts, one of which is handled at a time; when humanity has examined one part, it goes on to another; and so on. Whereas God is not subdivisible; he is a true whole, with no separable parts; each part is an aspect of the whole, and to know one " part " is to know implicitly all. The idea of progressive revelation is only a new materialism.

(*c*) Another objection of the same kind asserts that a man whose knowledge and will were divine in content would be himself only God-like, not actually one with God. He would be not identical but similar. This again depends on principles which we have already criticised. It is based on abstracting the personality of a mind from its content; I am I, whatever I do and say and think, and on the same terms you are you. The individual self-identity of the particular mind is unchangeable and underlies all changes of activity ; and therefore since A's ideas happen in A's mind and B's ideas in B's mind, A and B cannot have the same consciousness but only a similar one.

We have, as I said, already considered this view in detail. Our objection to it may be put shortly by saying that it admits at once too much and too little. If A's consciousness is only very like B's instead of being identical, there is no real communion between them ; for that requires an identity. But even this inadequate similarity cannot be maintained ; the same argument which destroyed the identity is fatal to it also. In fact this view is a compromise with materialism (in the form of psychological individualism or abstract pluralism), and any such compromise must be fatal to the whole truth.

(*d*) We must maintain, then, that it is possible for a human being to be identified with God in the concrete sense, as having a full and real intuition of the divine nature in its completeness, not of one side of it only, and a full harmony and agreement with the divine will ; not abandoning his own will and adopting the false negativity of quietism, but acting in complete union with God, so that where there might be two wills there is one, not by the annihilation of one but by the activity of both at once in a single purpose. Such a man would be rightly described as perfect God and perfect man, for the distinction would in his personality have no further meaning. He would therefore show in completion the powers of God in thought and in action.

This last statement may cause difficulty. It seems that the very fact of human life limits and circumscribes the man, and makes it impossible for him to exercise the full powers of the infinite mind of God. A particular man, it appears, cannot be omnipotent or omniscient, though he might be entirely sinless ; and therefore theories have arisen to the effect that in becoming man God would find it necessary to abandon certain of his attributes. Such a self-sacrifice seems to be an additional and very strong proof of the love of God towards humanity.

But it is not easy to see what can be meant by the renunciation of some of the divine attributes. The life of the mind is whole, without seam, woven from the top throughout; the only sense in which we can separate one attribute from the others is that we may abstract it, that is, have a false theory that is separate; we can never actually employ one faculty alone. The conception of the self-limitation of a will may in fact mean two things; either volition itself, which by accepting one end involves renunciation of another, or a volition in which it is determined not to will at all. Now in the former sense, self-limitation or self-sacrifice is the negative side of all acting; nothing can be done at all without the sacrifice of something else. Thus the temptation of Jesus, for instance, represents a true self-limitation; he decides not to adopt certain courses of action, not as a mere act of abstract self-sacrifice but because he is determined on a course with which these others are incompatible. In the second sense, self-limitation cannot exist at all; for every act of will is the will to do something, and a will, whose sole end was the abstract decision not to will, cannot be imagined. We never, strictly speaking, decide "not to do anything"; when we use that phrase we always mean that we decide not to do some definite thing A or B, but to go on doing C.

The self-limitation of God, then, cannot be interpreted in this abstract way as the mere renunciation of certain faculties. And it is not true that such things as omniscience and omnipotence are "faculties" at all, distinguishable from the faculties of knowing and acting in general. The question is whether human life as such is incompatible with the exercise of the divine attributes, wisdom and goodness, at all. No impassable gulf separates divine knowledge from human; God has not,

in addition to his power of knowing, another power
denied to man and called omniscience. Omniscience
is merely the name for the complete and unremitting
employment of the faculty of knowing. This faculty
man certainly possesses. If it were not so, the possibility of a divine-human life would doubtless be at an
end. Man could neither know God nor obey his will ;
and the divine spirit could only operate in man by losing
all its essential character. All human thought would
be illusion, and all human activity sin, and to make it
otherwise would be beyond the power of God himself.
Rather than accept such conclusions, we shall do right
in maintaining that all God's nature, without any reser-
vation or abatement, is expressible in human form.

The human being in whom God is fully manifested,
then, must have God's powers and faculties fully
developed, and if fully developed then fully employed,
since an unemployed faculty has no real existence at all.
He must be omnipotent and omniscient. Whatever
God can know and do, he also can know and do. This
is a grave difficulty if we think of omnipotence and
omniscience in an utterly abstract way, involving such
things as the power to make twice two into five or the
knowledge of an action which has not yet been decided
upon. But omnipotence does not mean power to do
absurdities. The compulsion of another's will is such
an absurdity ; and therefore no real omnipotence could
force such a compulsion. Omnipotence is spiritual, and
spirit acts not by brute compulsion but by knowledge
and inspiration. The omnipotence of God, his kingdom
over men's minds, consists in their allegiance to his
purposes, their answer to his love, their repentance and
return from sin to his side. And this omnipotence—
the universal kingdom which is planted in the hearts of
men—can indeed be wielded by God in human form.
To say that God cannot compel is not to deny him
omnipotence ; it is to assert his positive nature as spirit.
But since spirit is self-creative and makes its own nature,

this absence of compulsion is in one sense a self-limitation of the will of God. But (i.) it is a self-limitation of God as God, not of God as incarnate in man ; (ii.) it is only self-limitation in the sense in which any determination, *e.g.* of a good man to abstain from taking mean advantages, is a self-limitation.

In the category of knowledge we must also hold that the omniscience of God is shared by the Christ in whom his nature is manifested. It might be thought that this was unnecessary ; that the divine man would know God as he is, but would not know the things God knows. But such a plea is based on the false distinction between the mind and its content, the individual consciousness and the knowledge of which it is conscious. To know some one's mind is nothing more nor less than to see eye to eye with him, to look at reality as he looks at it, to know what he knows. His mind is not an object in itself ; it is an attitude towards the real world, and to know his mind is to know and share that attitude. The Christ, then, must be omniscient as God is.

This again is a serious difficulty. How can an individual man, whose consciousness is bounded by his age and time, be omniscient or even approximate to such a state? Is not that a fallacy now happily exploded and consigned to the theological rubbish-heap? Omniscient in a quite abstract sense the Christ cannot be, just as he cannot be in the same sense omnipotent. That is to say, looking at history as a succession of detached events temporally distinct, he cannot know the future ; future history, actions, and events generally he cannot foretell. But this is simply because, taking history in this abstract way, the future is positively undetermined, non-existent as yet, unknowable ; God himself cannot know it. On the other hand, if history means the discovery of absolute truth and the development of God's purposes, the divine man will stand at the centre of it and know it, past and future, from within, not as a process but as a whole. This means not that he will be acquainted with details of scholarship and history, but that he will know as from its source the essential truth at which wise men have aimed, so that whatever is of permanent value in knowledge, ancient or modern, is already summed up in his view of the world.

If God's purposes can be—as we have said—really hindered and blocked by evil wills, then God himself cannot know in advance their detailed history. He knows their ultimate fate ; he sees them as a composer sees his symphony complete and perfect ; but he cannot know beforehand every mistake of the performers. Those irruptions of the evil will into God's plans are no part of the unity of the world, no part of the plan ; it is only by destroying them, wiping them out of existence, that God's purposes can be fulfilled. God himself strives against evil, does not merely look down from heaven upon our conflict ; and if he does not blast the wicked with the breath of his mouth, neither does he set them up as mere puppets, targets for virtue's archery. The existence of evil, if it can be called a real abatement of God's omnipotence, is equally so of his omniscience ; not merely of that of his human manifestation. But as we said in a former chapter that evil does not truly limit God's omnipotence, because he conquers it in his own way, so the freedom of the future is not truly a detriment to his omniscience.

So far, then, it seems that the expression of deity in a human being is definitely possible, because in whatever sense we can conceive God to be omnipotent and omniscient, in the same sense it is conceivable that his human incarnation should be so. There will be no failure to express in bodily form the whole fulness of God's nature ; every aspect, every potentiality of his being will be included in the life of the perfect man who is also perfect God.

2. But if these are the relations of the Christ to

God, how shall we describe his relations with humanity ? In what sense can he be called perfect man, and what is the relation of his life and consciousness to those of the human race in general ?

(a) The first point is the reality of his manhood. There is a real difficulty in this point owing to the vagueness of the term " manhood." Many Christo-logical discussions suffer from lack of reflexion on this point. The conception of deity is thought to be a difficult and abstruse one, to elucidate which no pains are sufficient ; that of humanity, on the other hand, is often passed over as too simple to need investigation. Yet if we ask, Does a man who is identical with God thereby cease to be a man ? it is clear that he does or does not according to different senses of the word. Many people are ready to say that the notion of finitude, fallibility, sinfulness, is " contained in the very idea of manhood." If that is really so, then the perfect man cannot be called a man ; and any man becomes less and less human as he becomes better and better. If, on the other hand, we mean by man nothing more than a person living in human relations, then the perfect man is clearly a man among his fellow-men ; a better man, but a man. The question is what name we give to manhood purged of its imperfections ; and so far, it is a merely verbal question.

But the point at issue is not entirely verbal. Granted his divinity, his perfection and absoluteness, it may be said, he cannot be the member of a society in which every part is limited by and dovetailed into every other. He will burst the bonds of any society into which he is put ; and inasmuch as he is anti-social in this way he cannot be called a man among men. After what we have already said, this argument need not detain us long. It is true that he will certainly burst the bonds of any society, that his appearance heralds the overthrow of the world's powers, that he comes to bring a sword. But it is society that is anti-social, and not he ; he destroys it because of his humanity and its inhuman mechanisms and deadnesses. Destruction must always be the effect of any new truth or new impulse ; but what it destroys is man's idolatries, not man himself.

The most important difficulty in the way of conceiving the Christ as truly human is in the last resort identical with that which formed the subject of our last section (§1, *d*). As long as human and divine nature are regarded simply as different sets or groups of qualities, to assert their inherence in one individual is really meaningless, as if we should assert the existence of a geometrical figure which was both a square and a circle. This does not mean that those who asserted "two natures in one person" were wrong ; but it does mean that they were trying to express a truth in terms that simply would not express it. If any one said that he did not see how such a union of natures could take place, he was necessarily told that it was a mystery past understanding. But the mystery, the element which baffles the intellect, lies not at all in the truth to be expressed, but solely in its expression by improper language ; that is to say, the combination with it of presuppositions which contradict it. We start by assuming human nature to be one definite thing and divine nature another ; and the language which is framed on such a basis can never serve to express intelligibly the fact which it implicitly denies, namely the union of the two. This assumption we have by now criticised and found to be inadequate ; we have rejected the idea of a mind as having a "nature" of its own in distinction from what it does ; and by doing so we have removed in advance the abstract argument that a divine person, by his very nature, cannot be truly and completely human.

(*b*) But the impulse of the divine spirit is not exhausted by any one man. His followers, so far as they attain discipleship, share his spirit and his life ; his knowledge of God becomes theirs, and his identification of God's will with his own is also theirs. To this extent they have precisely the relation to him which he has to God ; and through him they attain the same relation to God in which he lives. That is to say, their mind actually becomes one with his mind, his mind lives in them and they in him. This must be true of every one who learns from him and follows him. The union with God which he enjoys is imparted to them ; they become he, and in so doing they equally with him become God.

Here again, we do not ask whether anybody has ever attained discipleship in this absolute degree ; we merely say that if any one did truly follow the light given by the divine incarnation he would live literally in God and God in him ; there would be no more " division of substance " than there is between the Father and the Son. Thus the Christ appears as Mediator of the divine life ; he enjoys that life to the full himself, and imparts it fully to his disciples. Through learning of him and following him it is possible to attain, by his mediation, the same divine life which we see in him.

(c) But such a union of life with life can hardly be confined to the definite disciples of any historical person. Among the countless numbers who know nothing of his life as a historic fact, to whom his words and example have never penetrated, are certainly many who have true knowledge of reality and the real attainment of a good life. What is the relation of these to the divine incarnation ?

The spirit of truth is not circumscribed by the limits of space and time. If a real community of life is possible between two men who share each other's outward presence and inward thoughts, it is possible no less between two who have never met ; between the ancient poet and his modern reader, or the dead scientist and the living man who continues his work. The earlier in point of time lives on in the life of the later ; each deriving the benefit from such intercourse. Even if we did not suppose the individual consciousness of the dead to remain with us, we should at least admit that all that was left of them—their work—profits by our carrying it on ; and we profit by using it as our starting-point. In this sense there is a real community between the Christ and the predecessors whose lives have, historically speaking, led up to and made possible his own.

Again, there is a union of mind between persons who are in the order of history unaware of each other's existence ; between Hebrew prophet and Greek philosopher ; between two scientists who cannot read each other's language. This union consists in the fact that both are dealing with the same problems ; for in so far as any two minds are conscious of the same reality, they are the same mind. Thus there is a certain spiritual intercourse between men who have no outward point of contact whatever ; and even if it is true, as Aristotle says, that bodily presence is the fulfilment of friendship, men may still be friends when neither knows the other's name.

The life of the Christ then is shared not only by his professed disciples but by all who know truth and lead a good life ; all such participate in the life of God and in that of his human incarnation. But whereas we say that his disciples enjoy the divine life through his mediation, it seems at first sight that we cannot speak of mediation in this other case. If mediation means simply example and instruction of one historical person by another, that is true. But there is no ultimate difference between the two cases. In each case the spirit of God, whose presence in the heart is truth, is shared by men as it was shared by the Christ ; and to speak of reaching him through God or God through him is to introduce a conception of process or transition which is really indefensible. As the disciple finds God in the Christ, so the non-disciple finds the Christ in God ; in the fact that he knows God he is already one with the Christ whom, "according to the flesh," he does not know.

M

The conception of mediation, then, does not stand in the last resort. The experience which it designates is perfectly real ; but the word itself implies a division of the indivisible. We speak of reaching God *through* Christ when we rather mean that we find him *in* Christ. And therefore the relation of the Christ to those who do not know him as a historical man is as intimate, granted that in their ignorance they do lead a life of truth and endeavour, as his union with those who call themselves his followers. In the language of religion, he saves not only his disciples but those who lived before his birth and those who never knew his name.

3. Whether such an incarnation has ever happened at all is, we repeat, a question for history. And if so, it is equally for history to decide whether it has happened once or many times. But on this question certain *a priori* points must be considered. There are certain arguments which seem to prove the plurality of incarnations.

(*a*) The first is the pantheistic argument. God is exemplified not simply in one man but in everything. There is no fact which does not reveal God to any one who is able to see him there. And consequently it is idle to talk of one final revelation. There are countless revelations.

This is almost a restatement of the view in § 1, *b*, which required an infinite number of revelations to express the infinite aspects of God's character. It springs from the thought that since God is all, every individual reality has an equal right to stand as a revelation of him. This is the view which we define as Pantheism. Our answer to that general position is that God is not every isolated thing, but only that which is good and true ; or, which comes, as we have seen, to the same thing, reality as a whole, in an ordered and coherent system. That which is good reveals God directly ; that which is evil reveals him indeed no less, but only indirectly, through its relations with the good.

A wicked man does not, by his wickedness, reveal the nature of God ; but if we understood the whole history, the beginning and end, of his sins, we should realise that he, no less than the good, stands as an example of God's dealings with the world.

(b) Secondly, there is a logical argument. God is regarded from this point of view as the universal, and man as the particular. Now every particular expresses the universal, and each expresses it completely. The whole universal is expressed in each particular, and the whole of the particular expresses the universal and nothing else. Every particular number is equally an example of number, and nothing but number. Therefore every man really expresses the universal, God, equally well. It may be that one particular expresses it to us more clearly than another by reason of certain conventionalities and habits of our mind ; as for instance a schoolboy might be unable to prove of a cardboard triangle what he can perfectly well prove of one in chalk on the blackboard. But this is a fault of the schoolboy, and no merit in the chalk triangle. One particular may seem to represent the universal in so uniquely perfect a way that it and it alone may be taken as the full representation of it; but this is never really a justifiable proceeding. It is a prejudice and an error.

On the other hand, the universal itself, which as a matter of fact exists only in various particulars, is sometimes falsely conceived as if it were itself another particular ; and thus arises the notion of an archetype or ideal specimen of a class, to which every less perfect member is an approximation. These two tendencies of false logic, the tendency to elevate one particular into the standard and only real instance of a universal, and the tendency to hypostasise the universal into a perfect and ideal particular, together give (it is supposed) the *rationale* of the process by which one man has been elevated into the sole and perfect revelation of the divine. The truth rather is (according to this view) that every man, as a particular instance of the nature of spirit, whose universal is God, is equally an instance of that nature and a manifestation of the essence of God.

This view is based on assuming that God is the universal of which man is the particular. But this can hardly be the case ; for God and man would then be as inseparable as triangularity from a given triangle. The fact of evil, that is to say, the alienation of man from God, becomes on such a view mere nonsense, as if one should talk of the de-triangularising of triangles. The assumption involved, that every man as such is completely and in the fullest sense divine, begs the question at issue. Indeed it is an unwarranted assumption that because we call a given set of individuals men therefore they equally well manifest even the nature of men. If human nature means virtues—what man ought to be—it is not common to every man equally. Some men in that sense are human and others inhuman. And if it merely means the bare qualities which every man has in common, such qualities considered in abstraction are nothing definite at all ; for the quality which one man makes a means to crime another may use as a means to virtue ; and the crime or the virtue are the really important things, the character of the individual men. But these are not common to all men, and therefore not " human nature " in this sense. In fact there is no such thing as human nature in the sense of a definite body of characteristics common to every one, and if there were it would not be by any means the same thing as God.

If the universal is a quality or attribute exemplified by individuals which are called its particulars, according to the doctrine of logic, then the relation between God and men is not one of universal and particular. If God were considered as simply the quality goodness instead of being a person, then he would be the universal of all good actions ; but on that account he would not be the universal of bad ones, and since bad actions are real acts of will, God would not be the universal of minds as such. The ordinary logical conception of the universal, the one quality of many things, is in fact inapplicable to the relation between God and other minds. And therefore we cannot argue that any particular mind shows the nature of God as well as any other. The question to be asked about mind is not what it is, but what it does ; a question with which the logic of things and qualities does not deal.

(c) Beyond these objections the question of Christ's uniqueness passes into the region of history. It is only necessary to add one warning : that if he is the means of communicating the divine life to man and raising man into union with God, the very success of his mission will in one sense destroy his uniqueness. Any one who fully learns his teacher's lesson has become spiritually one with his teacher ; and therefore the teacher's experience of the truth is no longer unique. The teacher remains unique only as the first discoverer of the truth in the order of time, or as the mediator of it in the order of education ; in the completion of his life this uniqueness disappears into absolute unity with his disciples. If therefore we try to define the uniqueness of the Christ in such a way as to make his experience incapable of real communication to man, we shall be preserving his divinity at the expense of his humanity, and making the supposed manifestation of God to man an illusion. The revelation — any revelation — sets before us an ideal ; if the ideal is not literally and completely capable of attainment, it is not an ideal at all. It is an *ignis fatuus.*

But if this is so, it will be asked, why does history tell us of one and only one life in which it has been fully attained ? Does not the isolated position of Jesus Christ in history, his infinite moral superiority to all the saints, prove that there was in his nature some element that is denied to us ; and are we not driven by the facts to suppose that his uniqueness lay not so much in the use he made of human faculties as in the possession of superhuman ?

To this we must reply that the possession by any person of faculties inherently different, whether in nature or integrity, from our own, makes our attempts to live his life not merely vain but unreasonable ; as if a man should emulate the strength of an elephant or a hereditary consumptive the physique of his untainted ancestors. If it is answered that these higher faculties can indeed be possessed by man, but only as bestowed by divine grace, we shall reply that this is exactly the position we have been maintaining : for we believe that a man's human nature consists in no definite and circumscribed group of qualities, but precisely in those achievements to which the divine grace may lead him, or those sins into which he may fall by the rejection of such guidance. But to explain why one man attains and another fails is no part of our task.

(*d*) The Christ has absolute experience of the nature of God and lives in absolute free obedience to his will. So far as anybody attains these ideals in the pursuit of truth and duty, he shares the experience with Christ in absolute union with him, that is, with God. Such moments of attainment, in even the greatest men, are no doubt rare ; but they are the metal of life which, when the reckoning is made, is separated from the dross and is alone worth calling life at all. Separate out from the total of experience all errors, all failures, all sins ; and the gold that is left will be entirely one with the Christ-life. We thus see from a new point of view the absolute unity of Christ and God ; for, as we said earlier, God is the reality of the world conceived as a whole which in its self-realisa-tion and impulse towards unity purges out of itself all evil and error. History regarded in that way—not as a mere bundle of events but as a process of the solution of problems and the overcoming of difficulties—is altogether summed up in the infinite personality of

God ; and we can now see that it is equally summed up in the infinite personality of the God-Man.

If Christ is thus the epitome, the summary and ordered whole, of history, the same is true of every man in his degree. The attainment of any real truth is an event, doubtless, in time, and capable of being catalogued in the chronologies of abstract history ; but the truth itself is not historically circumscribed. A man may come to know God through a sudden "revelation" or "conversion" ; but God is the same now and for ever. In the knowledge of God, then, which means in all true knowledge, man comes into touch with something out of time, something to which time makes no difference. And since knowledge of God is union with God, he does not merely see an extra-temporal reality ; he does not merely glance through breaking mists at the battlements of eternity, as Moses saw the promised land from the hill of renunciation. By his knowledge of eternity he is one with eternity ; he has set himself in the centre of all time and all existence, free from the changes and the flux of things. He has entered into the life of God, and in becoming one with God he is already beyond the shadow of changing and the bitterness of death.

There is a faint analogue to this immortality in the work by which a man leaves something of himself visibly present on earth. The workman in a cathedral sets his own mark upon the whole and leaves his monument in the work of his hands. He passes away, but his work—his expressed thought, his testimony to the glory of God—remains enshrined in stone. Even that is liable to decay, and in time such earthly immortality is as if it had never been. But if a man has won his union with the mind of God, has known God's thought and served God's purpose in any of the countless ways in which it can be served, his monument is not something that stands for an age when he is dead.

It is his own new and perfected life ; something that in its very nature cannot pass away, except by desertion of the achieved ideal. This is the statue of the perfect man, more perennial than bronze ; the life in a house not made with hands, eternal in the heavens.

CHAPTER II

1. WHATEVER else is involved in the doctrine of the Atonement, it includes at least this : that the sins of man are forgiven by God. And here at the very outset a difficulty arises which must be faced before the doctrine can be further developed. Forgiveness and punishment are generally conceived as two alternative ways of treating a wrongdoer. We may punish any particular criminal, or we may forgive him ; and the question always is, which is the right course of action. On the one hand, however, punishment seems to be not a conditional but an absolute duty ; and to neglect it is definitely wrong. Justice in man consists at least in punishing the guilty, and the conception of a just God similarly emphasises his righteous infliction of penalties upon those who break his laws. The very idea of punishment is not that it is sometimes right and sometimes wrong or indifferent, but that its infliction is an inexorable demand of duty.

On the other hand, forgiveness is presented as an equally vital duty for man and an equally definite characteristic of God. This, again, is not conditional. The ideal of forgiveness is subject to no restrictions. The divine precept does not require us to forgive, say, seven times and then turn on the offender for reprisals. Forgiveness must be applied unequivocally to every offence alike.

Here, then, we have an absolute contradiction

between two opposing ideals of conduct. And the result of applying the antithesis to the doctrine of atonement is equally fatal whichever horn of the dilemma is accepted. Either punishment is right and forgiveness wrong, or forgiveness is right and punishment wrong. If punishment is right, then the doctrine that God forgives our sins is illusory and immoral ; it ascribes to God the weakness of a doting father who spares the rod and spoils the child. If punishment is wrong, then the conception of a punishing God is a mere barbarism of primitive theology, and atonement is no mystery, no divine grace, but simply the belated recognition by theology that its God is a moral being. Thus regarded, the Atonement becomes either a fallacy or a truism.

And it is common enough, in the abstract and hasty thought which in every age passes for modern, to find the conception of atonement dismissed in this way. But such thought generally breaks down in two different directions. In its cavalier treatment of a doctrine, it ignores the real weight of thought and experience that has gone to the development of the theory, or broadly condemns it as illusion and dreams ; and secondly, it proceeds without sufficient speculative analysis of its own conceptions, with a confidence based in the last resort upon ignorance. The historian of thought will develop the first of these objections ; our aim is to consider the second.

The dilemma which has been applied to theology must, of course, equally apply to moral or political philosophy. In order to observe it at work, we must see what results it produces there. Punishment and forgiveness are things we find in our own human society ; and unless we are to make an end of theology, religion, and philosophy by asserting that there is no relation between the human and the divine, we must try to explain each by what we know of the other.

(*a*) The first solution of the dilemma, then, might be

to maintain that punishment is an absolute duty and forgiveness positively wrong. We cannot escape the rigour of this conclusion by supposing forgiveness to be "non-moral," for we cannot evade moral issues; the possibility of forgiveness only arises in cases where punishment is also an alternative, and if punishment is always right, then forgiveness must always be a crime.

Forgiveness, on this view, is a sentimental weakness, a mere neglect of the duty to punish. It is due to misguided partiality towards an offender; and instead of cancelling or wiping out his crime, endorses it by committing another. Now this is a view which might conceivably be held; and if consistently held would be difficult to refute, without such a further examination of the conceptions involved as we shall undertake later. At this stage we can only point out that it does not deserve the name of an ethical theory; because it emphasises one fact in the moral consciousness and arbitrarily ignores others. The fact is that people do forgive, and feel that they are acting morally in so doing. They distinguish quite clearly in their own minds between forgiving a crime and sentimentally overlooking or condoning it. Now the theory does not merely ignore this fact, but it implicitly or even, if pressed, explicitly denies it. To a person who protested "But I am convinced that it is a duty to forgive," it would reply, "Then you are wrong; it is a crime." And if asked why it is a crime, the theory would explain, "Because it is inconsistent with the duty to punish." But the duty to punish rests on the same basis as the duty to forgive; it is a pronouncement of the moral consciousness. All the theory does is to assume quite uncritically that the moral consciousness is right in the one case and wrong in the other; whereas the reverse is equally possible. The two duties may be contradictory, but they rest on the same basis; and the argument which discredits one discredits the other too.

(*b*) The same difficulty applies to the other horn of

the dilemma, according to which forgiveness is always right and punishment always wrong. Just as we cannot say that forgiveness is a crime because punishment is a duty, so we cannot say that punishment is a crime because forgiveness is a duty. But the theory of the immorality of punishment has been worked out rather more fully than is (I believe) the case with the theory of the immorality of forgiveness.

(i.) Just as forgiveness was identified with sentimental condoning of an offence, so punishment has been equated with personal revenge. This view has been plausibly expressed in terms of evolution by the hypothesis that revenge for injuries has been gradually, in the progress of civilisation, organised and centralised by state control ; so that instead of a vendetta we nowadays have recourse to a lawsuit as our means of reprisal on those who have done us wrong. But such a statement over-looks the fact that punishment is not revenge in the simple and natural sense of that word. The difference is as plain as that between forgiveness and the neglect of the duty to punish. Revenge is a second crime which does nothing to mitigate the first ; punishment is not a crime but something which we feel to be a duty. The " state organisation of revenge " really means the annihilation or supersession of revenge and the substitution for it of equitable punishment. And if we ask how this miracle has happened, the only answer is that people have come to see that revenge is wrong and so have given it up.

(ii.) A less crude theory of punishment as merely selfish is the view which describes it as deterrent, as a means of self-preservation on the part of society. We are told that crime in general is detrimental to social well-being (or, according to more thorough-going forms of the conception, what is found to be detrimental is arbitrarily called crime), and therefore society inflicts certain penalties on criminals in order to deter them and others from further anti-social acts. It is the function of "justice" to determine what amount of terror is necessary in order to prevent the crime.

Punishment so explained is not moral. We punish not because it is a duty but because it preserves us against certain dangers. A person has done us an injury, and we maltreat him, not out of a spirit of revenge, far from it, but in order to frighten others who may wish to imitate him. The condemned criminal is regarded as a marauder nailed *in terrorem* to the barn-door. One feels inclined to ask how such a combination of cruelty and selfishness can possibly be justified in civilised societies ; and if the theory is still possessed by a lingering desire to justify punishment, it will perhaps reply that the criminal has " forfeited his right " to considerate treatment. Which means either that he has cut himself off from our society altogether (which he plainly has not) or that there is nothing wrong in being cruel to a criminal ; which is monstrous. If society is trying to be moral at all, it has duties towards a criminal as much as towards any one else. It may deny the duties, and have its criminals eaten by wild beasts for its amusement, or tortured for its increased security ; perhaps the former is the less revolting practice ; but in either case society is demonstrating its own corruption.

The deterrent theory, then, must not be used as a justification, but only as an impeachment, of punishment. But even if punishment is, as the theory maintains, a purely selfish activity, it must still be justified in a sense; not by its rightness but by its success. The question therefore is whether as a matter of fact punishment does deter. Now a "just" penalty, on this theory, is defined as one which is precisely sufficient to deter. If it does not deter, it is condemned as giving insufficient protection to society, and therefore unjust. Society will accordingly increase it, and this increase will continue till a balance is established and the crime is stamped out. Those crimes therefore happen oftenest whose statutable penalties are most in defect of this ideal balance. The fact that they happen proves that the penalty is inadequate. Therefore, if the deterrent view is correct, society must be anxious to increase these penalties. But we do not find that this is the case. If criminal statistics show an increase, we do not immediately increase the penalties. Still less do we go on increasing them further and further until the crime is no longer attractive. If we may argue from empirical evidence, such as the infliction of the death-penalty for petty thefts, it is simply not the case that increased severity necessarily diminishes crime; and yet on the theory it ought to do so. On the contrary, it sometimes appears that higher penalties go with greater frequency. To reply to this that the frequency of crime is the cause, not the effect, of the greater severity, would be to confess the failure of punishment as deterrent ; for, on that view, severity ought to be the *cause* of *infrequency*, not the *effect* of *frequency*. The plea would amount to a confession that we cannot, as is supposed, control the amount of crime by the degree of punishment.

Thus the view that punishment is a selfish act of society to secure its own safety against crime breaks down. Its plausibility depends on the truth that the severity of punishments is somehow commensurate with the badness of the crime ; that there is a connexion of degree between the two. If we ask how this equation is brought about, the theory disappears at once. In punishment we do not try to hurt a man as much as he has hurt us ; or even as much as may induce him not to hurt us. The "amount" of punishment is fixed by one standard only ; what we suppose him to deserve. This is difficult to define exactly, and common practice represents only a very rough approximation to it ; but it is that, not anything else, at which the approximation aims. And the conception of desert reintroduces into punishment the moral criterion which the theory tried to banish from it. To aim at giving a man the punishment he deserves implies that he does deserve it, and therefore that it is our duty to give it him.

(c) Both these escapes, therefore, have failed. We cannot say that either punishment or forgiveness is wrong, and thus vindicate the necessity of the other. Though contradictory they are both imperative. Nor can we make them apply to different cases; maintaining for instance that we should forgive the repentant and punish the obdurate. If we only forgive a man after he has repented, that is to say, put away his guilt and become good once more, the idea of forgiveness is a mockery. The very conception of forgiveness is that it should be our treatment of the guilty as guilty.

Nor can we escape by an abstraction distinguishing the sinner from the sin. We punish not the sin, but the sinner for his sin ; and we forgive not the sinner distinguished from his sin, but identified with it and manifested in it. If we punish the sin, we must forgive the sin too : if we forgive the sinner, we must equally punish him.

2. This absolute contradiction between the two duties can only be soluble in one way. A contradiction of any kind is soluble either by discovering one member of it to be false, an expedient which has already been tried, or by showing that the two are not really, as we had supposed, incompatible. This is true, whether the contradiction is between two judgments of fact or between two duties or so-called "judgments of value"; for if it is axiomatic that two contradictory judgments cannot both be true, it is equally axiomatic that two incompatible courses of action cannot both be obligatory. This fact may be obscured by saying that on certain occasions we are faced with two alternatives of which each is a duty, but the question is which is the greater duty. But the "greater duty" is a phrase without meaning. In the supposed case the distinction is between this which we ought to do, and that which we ought not ; the distinction between *ought* and *ought not* is not a matter of degree.

Granted, then, that in any given situation there can be only one duty, it follows necessarily that if of two actions each is really obligatory the two actions must be the same. We are therefore compelled to hold that punishment and forgiveness, so far from being incompatible duties, are really when properly understood identical. This may seem impossible ; but as yet we have defined neither conception, and this we must now proceed to do.

(a) Punishment consists in the infliction of deserved suffering on an offender. But it is not yet clear what suffering is inflicted, and how it is fixed, beyond the bare fact that it must be deserved. If we ask, Why is that particular sort and amount of pain inflicted on this particular man? the answer, "That is what he deserves," no doubt conveys the truth, but it does not fully explain it. It is not immediately clear without further thought that *this* must be the right punishment. Punishment is fixed not by a self-evident and inexplicable intuition, but by some motive or process of thought which we must try to analyse. The conception of desert proves that this motive is moral ; and it remains to ask what is the moral attitude towards a crime or criminal.

If we take the case of a misdeed of our own and consider the attitude of our better moments towards it, we see that this attitude is one of condemnation. It is the act of a good will declaring its hostility to a bad one. This feeling of rejection, condemnation, or hostility is in fact the necessary attitude of all good wills towards all evil acts. The moral action of the person who punishes, therefore, consists primarily in this condemnation. Further, the condemnation, in our own case, is the act in and through which we effect our liberation or alienation from the evil, and our adherence to the good. If a person is in a state of sin, that he should feel hostility towards his own sin is necessary to his moral salvation ; he cannot become good except by condemning his own crime. The condemnation of the crime is not the *means* to goodness; it *is* the manifestation of the new good will.

The condemnation of evil is the necessary manifestation of all good wills. If A has committed a crime, B, if he is a moral person, condemns it. And this condemnation he will express to A if he is in social relations with him ; for social relations consist of sharing thoughts and activities so far as possible. If B is successful in communicating his condemnation to A, A will thereupon share it ; for A's knowledge that B condemns him, apart from his agreement in the condemnation, is not really a case of communication. But if A shares the condemnation he substitutes in that act a good will for an evil. The process is now complete ; A's sin, B's condemnation, B's expression to A of his feelings, A's conversion and repentance. This is the inevitable result of social relations between the two persons, granting that A's will is good and that the relations are maintained.

Now this self-expression of a good will towards a bad is, I think, what we mean by the duty of punishment. It is no doubt the case that we describe many things as punishment in which we can hardly recognise these features at all. But examination of such cases shows that precisely so far as these facts are not present, so far as the punishment does not express moral feelings, and does not aim in some degree at the self-conviction of the criminal—so far, we are inclined to doubt whether it is a duty at all, and not a convention, a farce, or a crime. We conclude, therefore, that punishment—the only punishment we can attribute to God or to a good man—is the expression to a criminal of the punisher's moral attitude towards him. Hence punishment is an absolute duty ; since not to feel that attitude would be to share his crime, and not to express it would be a denial of social relations, an act of hypocrisy.

(*b*) The pain inflicted on the criminal, then, is not the pain of evil consequences, recoiling from his action in the course of nature or by the design of God or man

N

upon his own head ; still less is it the mere regret for having done something which involves himself or others in such consequences.   These things are not punishment at all, and ought never to be confused with it, though they may well be incidental to it.   The pain of punishment is simply the pain of self-condemnation or moral repentance ; the renunciation of one aim and the turning of the will to another.   That is what we try to inflict upon him ; and any other, incidental pains are merely the means by which we express to him our attitude and will.   But why, it may be asked, should these incidental pains be necessary ?   Why should they be the only means of communicating such feelings ?   The answer is that they are not.   The most perfect punishments involve no "incidental" pains at all.   The condemnation is expressed simply and quietly in words, and goes straight home.   The punishment consists in expression of condemnation and that alone ; and to punish with a word instead of a blow is still punishment. It is, perhaps, a better and more civilised form of punishment ; it indicates a higher degree of intelligence and a more delicate social organisation.   If a criminal is extremely coarsened and brutalised, we have to express our feelings in a crude way by cutting him off from the privileges of a society to whose moral aims he has shown himself hostile ; but if we are punishing a child, the tongue is a much more efficient weapon than the stick.

Nor does the refinement of the penalty end there. It is possible to punish without the word of rebuke ; to punish by saying nothing at all, or by an act of kindness.   Here again, we cannot refuse the name of punishment because no "physical suffering" is inflicted. The expression of moral feelings, or the attitude of the good will to the bad, may take any form which the wrongdoer can understand.   In fact, it is possible to hold that we often use "strong measures" when a word or a kind action would do just as well, or better.   "If thine enemy hunger, feed him; for in so doing thou shalt heap coals of fire on his head." Sentimentalists have recoiled in horror from such a refinement of brutality, not realising that to heap coals of fire, the fires of repentance, upon the head of the wrongdoer is the desire of all who wish to save his soul, not to perpetuate and endorse his crime.

But at this stage of the conception we should find it hard to discriminate between punishment and forgiveness. If punishment is to express condemnation, it must be the condemnation of a bad will by a good one. That is to say, it is the self-expression of a good will, and that good will is expressed as truly in the act of kindness as in the block and gallows. But if the punisher's will really is good, he continues, however severe his measures, to wish for the welfare and regeneration of the criminal. He punishes him not wholly with a view to " his good," because the punishment is not consciously undertaken as a means to an end, but as the spontaneous expression of a moral will ; yet the aim of that will is not the criminal's mutilation or suffering as such but the awakening of his moral consciousness. And to treat the criminal as a fellow-man capable of reformation, to feel still one's social relation and duty towards him, is surely the attitude which we call forgiveness.

If forgiveness means remission of the penalty, it is impossible to a moral will. For the penalty is simply the judgment ; it is the expression of the moral will's own nature. If forgiveness means the remission of the more violent forms of self-expression on the part of the good will, then such restraint is not only still punishment but may be the most acute and effective form of it. But if forgiveness means—as it properly does—the wise and patient care for the criminal's welfare, for his regeneration and recovery into the life of a good society, then there is no distinction whatever between forgiveness and punishment.

(c) Punishment and forgiveness are thus not only

compatible but identical ; each is a name for the one and only right attitude of a good will towards a man of evil will. The details of the self-expression vary according to circumstances ; and when we ask, " Shall we punish this man or forgive him ? " we are really considering whether we shall use this or that method of expressing what is in either case equally punishment and forgiveness. The only important distinction we make between the two words is this : they refer to the same attitude of mind, but they serve to distinguish it from different ways of erring. When we describe an attitude as one of forgiveness, we mean to distinguish it, as right, from that brutality or unintelligent severity (punishment falsely so called) which inflicts pain either in mere wantonness or without considering the possibility of a milder expression. When we call it punishment, we distinguish it as right from that weakness or sentimentality (forgiveness falsely so called) which by shrinking from the infliction of pain amounts to condonation of the original offence.

3. The identity of punishment and forgiveness removes the preliminary difficulty in the way of any doctrine of atonement. So far as we can now understand God's attitude towards sin, it may be expressed thus.

God's attitude towards the sins of men must be one which combines condemnation of the sinful will with love and hope for it ; these two being combined not as externally connected and internally inconsistent elements of a state of mind, but as being the single necessary expression of his perfect nature towards natures less perfect, but regarded as capable of perfection. This attitude on the part of God is, further, the means of man's redemption ; for by understanding God's attitude towards sin man comes himself to share in that attitude, and is thus converted to a new life in harmony with God's good will.

Here we seem to have a relation involving two

separate activities, the divine and the human. On the one hand there is the initiation of the repentance, the act of punishment or forgiveness on the part of God ; and on the other, the response to God's act, the repentance of man in virtue of the original self-expression of God.

These are two inseparable aspects of one and the same process ; the tendency to lay exclusive emphasis on one or the other leads to two main types of theory, each equally unsatisfactory because each, while really one-sided, claims to be an account of the whole truth. These views I call the objective and subjective theories respectively.

(a) The objective theory of atonement points out that whatever change takes place in the human will is due to the free gift of the Spirit of God. Man can do nothing good except by virtue of God's grace, and therefore if the evil will of a man is converted into a good will, the whole process is an act of God. The Atonement, the redemption of man, is a fact entirely on the side of God, not at all on the side of man ; for without God's help and inspiration there would be nothing good in man at all.

This view lays the emphasis on God's attitude to the world ; and concerns itself chiefly with the question, What change did the Incarnation mark in the development of God's plans ? We cannot suppose that there was no change at all, that it merely put a new ideal before man, because man always had high ideals ; he had Moses and the prophets, and had not listened to them. The divine grace of the Atonement consists in the imparting not of a new ideal but of a new power and energy to live up to the ideal. Man, in a word, cannot redeem himself ; his redemption comes from God and is God's alone.

Now this " objective " view is exposed to the danger of forgetting that redemption must be the redemption of a will, the change of a will ; and that in the last resort a will can only be changed by itself. If this is forgotten, the objective theory lapses into an abstract legalism according to which grace becomes a fictitious and conventional restoration to favour without any corresponding renovation of character. These two things must never be allowed to fall apart in such a way that the Atonement consists in one to the exclusion of the other ; for unless the grace of God awakes a response in the will of man there is no true atonement. But this response is just the fact which this type of theory tends either to overlook or at least to describe with insufficient accuracy.

In examining actual theories of the Atonement, however, we must bear in mind that a verbal statement which appears to be one-sided does not necessarily either neglect or exclude the other side. The objective view is perfectly true so far as it goes ; and the criticism often directed against it, on the ground that redemption is a matter of the individual will alone and must arise entirely from within, is due to a fallacious theory of personality.

(*b*) The "subjective" theory insists on the attitude of man to God, and lays down that since redemption involves an attitude or state of the subject's will it cannot without violence to his freedom be brought about by the act of another person, even if that other person be God. Grace as something merely proceeding from God is not only a hypothesis, but a useless hypothesis ; the fact to be explained is the change, repentance, reformation of the individual, and this fact cannot be explained by reference to another's actions. Nobody can change my mind for me except myself. The question in short is not, What change has occurred in God ?—since God is and always was long-suffering and merciful. It is rather, What difference has the life of Christ made in me ? How has his example fired me to imitate him, his life challenged me to new effort, his love called forth love in me ?

This view is attended by a parallel danger. It insists on the reality and inviolability of the individual ; and the least over-emphasis on this truth leads to the theory that no real help, no real stimulus, can pass over from one individual to another. In short, it brings us to the exclusive or individualistic theory of personality for which every person is a law to himself, supplies himself with his own standards of right and wrong, and draws upon his own resources in order to live up to them ; for which the influence of one person on another is either impossible or—inconsistently with the theory— possible, but an "infringement of the rights" of the individual. From such a point of view it might be replied to one who spoke of Christ's life on earth, " What good can it do ? He lived nobly, you say, and died a martyr ; but why should you tell me these things ? I can only do what lies in my power; I cannot behave like a hero, being the man I am. It is useless for you to set up an ideal before me unless you can give me strength to live up to it. And the strength that I do not possess nobody can give me." And if the instructor goes on to expound the doctrine of grace and the indwelling of the Spirit of the Lord in his Church, the reply will be that these things are dreams ; impossible from the very nature of personality, which is such that "one consciousness"—that of the Holy Spirit—"cannot include another"—that of an individual human being ; or else that if these things are possible they involve an intolerable swamping of one's own personality, a surrender of one's freedom and individuality which can only be a morbid and unhealthy state of mind.

We have dealt with this individualistic theory elsewhere, and shall now only repeat that it implies the negation not merely of atonement in the sense of redemption of man whether by man, Christ, or God, but also of social life as a whole ; and therefore destroys by implication the very individual whose reality it hoped to vindicate. It presents us with the portrait of an ideal man who stands in no need of any external stimulus or assistance in working out his own salvation. If such a person existed, he would be independent of God and man alike, and would justly feel insulted by the offer of an atonement. But the portrait is untrue, not simply because no actual man ever attains this complete self-dependence, but rather because it is a false ideal ; the perfect life for man is a life not of absolute isolation but of absolute communion. A man shows his greatness not in ignoring his surroundings but in understanding and assimilating them ; and his debt to his environment is no loss to his individuality but a gain.

(*c*) It must be obvious by now that of the two theories sketched above, each is an abstraction ; each emphasises one side of a reality in which both sides are present and in which, as a matter of fact, both sides are one. The two sides must be united ; but this cannot be effected by a compromise. A compromise is a middle path between two extremes, and includes neither. The combination at which we must aim will assert both theories to the full while avoiding the errors which alone keep them apart. As often happens in such cases, the two opposing theories are based on the same error, and a little further analysis will show wherein this error consists.

The danger of objectivism was to assume that grace could pass from God to man leaving man's inmost will untouched. The legalistic conception of grace depended on the separation of the human personality from the divine as two vessels, one of which might receive " content " from the other while its nature remained unaltered. The theory clings to the omnipotence of God and the fact that from him comes man's salvation, but conceives this omnipotence as God's power of imposing his own good will upon man. But this is no true redemption ; the man's own will is merely superseded by, not unified with, the will of God. That is to say the good will which is manifested is solely God's and not in any sense man's. The human will is not redeemed but annihilated.

In order to avoid this conclusion subjectivism lays stress on the point which the above theory was led to deny, namely the fact that redemption is a free state of man's own will. It rightly asserts that whatever reform takes place in the character must be the work of the character itself, and cannot be thrust upon it by the operation of another. But it goes on to deny that redemption is in any sense the work of God, and to maintain that no act of God can have any influence on the moral destiny of man. Thus the conception of a divine will disappears altogether from the world of human morality.

The implication in each case seems to be the same ; for to assert the will of God and deny man's inner redemption, or to assert man's redemption and deny the will of God, equally implies conceiving God's power and man's freedom to be inconsistent. This is the fallacy common to the two views. Each alike holds that a given action may be done either by God or by man, in either case the other being inactive. This separation of the will of God from that of man is fatal to any theory of the Atonement, where the fact to be explained is that man is redeemed not merely by his own act but also and essentially by God's.

A satisfactory theory of the Atonement seems to demand that the infusion of grace from God does not forcibly and artificially bring about but actually is a change of mind in man. It is an event which only co-operation of the various wills involved can effect at all. The error of the objective theory (or rather the error into which that way of stating the truth is most liable to fall) is to regard God as wholly active, man as wholly passive ; and to forget that God's purpose of redemption is powerless apart from man's will to be redeemed.

The tendency of subjectivism on the other hand is to assume that the righteousness of man is independent of his relation to God ; that man's will is sanctified by his own effort whether he is justified in the eyes of God or not.   Here again the fault lies in the absolute separation of man from God.   God is not realised as the one and only source of goodness ; it is not understood that to will the right is to unify one's will with God's.   The two things—righteousness and reconciliation with God —are really one and the same, and to represent one as means to the other or *vice versa*, or to insist on one and neglect the other, implies forgetting their identity and making an arbitrary and false separation of the two.

Neither is it enough merely to combine the two sides which the foregoing theories have separated.   That would be to make the Atonement a combination of two different acts—God's forgiveness and man's repentance —of which each is peculiar to its own agent ; it would fail to account for the essential unity of the whole process, and, taking the two sides as co-ordinate and equally vital, would substitute an unintelligible dualism for what is really one fact.   In other words, any theory must show exactly how the forgiveness of God is related to the repentance of man ; how it is possible for the one to bring about the other ; and the dualistic view would be nothing more than a restatement of this central difficulty.

The failure of the theories hitherto examined has been in every case due to this distinction within the Atonement of two sides, God's and man's.   Each agent, it is supposed, makes his own individual contribution to the whole process ; God's contribution being the act of forgiveness, man's that of repentance.   Now our previous analysis of the idea of co-operation suggests that this distinction needs revising.   We found in a former chapter that in the co-operation of two wills we could only disentangle the respective contribution to the whole of each separate personality by an act of forcible and arbitrary abstraction ; that in point of fact the two minds became identified in a common experience of which each willed the whole and neither a mere part.

If we mean to apply this principle to the present difficulty, we must find a statement of the case which will
no longer distinguish God's contribution from man's ;
which will enable us to say that God's punishment of
man is man's own self-punishment, and that man's
repentance is God's repentance too. If we can hold
such a view we shall have identified the part played by
God in redemption with that played by man ; and we
shall be able to define the Atonement, in terms consistent with our general theory, as the re-indwelling of
the divine spirit in a man who has previously been
alienated from it.

4. We have to make two identifications ; first to
show that God's punishment of man is man's punishment
of himself, and second that man's repentance is God's
repentance also.

The first point causes little difficulty after our
examination of the meaning of punishment. We have
already seen that the essence of punishment is the communication to the offender of our condemnation of his
act ; and that therefore all punishment consists in trying
to make a criminal punish himself, that is inflict on
himself the pain of remorse and conversion from his
evil past to a better present.   It is clear therefore without
further explanation that in God's punishment of sin the
sinner, through repentance, punishes his own sin.   God's
activity is shared by man too ; man co-operates with
God in punishing himself.   And just as he punishes
himself, he forgives himself, for he displays in repentance
just that combination of severity towards the past and
hope towards the future in which true forgiveness
consists.

(a) The conception of divine repentance is at first
sight less easy to grasp ; but this is because we have
not yet asked what is the precise nature of the experience
to which we attach the name.   We are in the habit of
defining repentance as the conversion of an evil will to
good ; a condition only possible to one who has been

sinful and is in process of renouncing his own sin.   And
if we accept this definition as final, we can only say that
the conception of divine penitence is self-contradictory.
Repentance is peculiar to a sinner ; God is not a sinner,
therefore he cannot feel repentance.

But we must ask whether the account offered of
repentance is really satisfactory.   Repentance is a
particular state of mind, a feeling of a quite individual
kind ; and it is notoriously difficult to define a feeling
in so many words.   In point of fact, we generally give
up the attempt, and substitute for a definition of the
thing itself a description of the circumstances in which
we feel it.   If we are asked what we mean by the
feelings of triumph, sorrow, indignation and so on, we
reply as a rule by explaining the kind of occasion which
excites them : " triumph is what you feel when you
have succeeded in spite of opposition."   But this is
quite a different thing from stating what triumph feels
like.   This method of description is very common.
We apply it for instance to such things as smells, for
which we have practically no descriptive vocabulary.
We generally define a scent not by its individual nature
but by its associations ; we state not what sort of smell
it is but what it is the smell of.

Definition by circumstances (as we may call it) is apt
to mislead us seriously in any attempt to describe our
feelings.   We think we have described the feeling when
we have only described the occasions on which it arises;
and since in consequence of this habit we apply names to
feelings rather in virtue of their occasions than because
of their own characters, we are often ready to assert
a priori who can and who cannot experience a given
emotion, merely on the ground that if such and such a
person felt it we should call it something else.

In the case of repentance we are being misled by
words if we argue that repentance is the conversion of a
sinful will and therefore impossible to God.   Repentance
is a perfectly definite feeling with a perfectly definite

character of its own: when we experience it, we recognise it as we recognise a smell, not because of any external circumstances but simply because of something which we may call its own peculiar flavour.   In asking whether a sinless person feels repentance we must try to fix our minds on this flavour, not on its external associations.

We must notice that even the occasion of repentance has not been very well described.   Its occasion is not the mere abstract point of junction, so to speak, between two states, a bad state and a good state.   We do not cease to repent when our will becomes good.   Indeed if that were the case we should never repent at all ; for the moment of transition from a bad will to a good is not a positive experience ; it is the mere chink or joint between two experiences.   Conversion is not a neutral moment between being bad and being good ; it is a feeling set up by the inrush of positive goodness. Repentance, then, must be re-defined by its circumstances as the peculiar feeling of a converted person towards his own evil past.   A person only repents in so far as he is now good ; repentance is necessarily the attitude of a good will.   It does not precede conversion ; it is the spirit of conversion.

If repentance is the feeling with which a person contemplates the evil past he has left behind him, the problem is to distinguish it from the feeling with which he, or any good person, contemplates the misdeeds of another.   If we can maintain such a distinction, we cannot admit the reality of divine penitence.

Now if we look at the matter solely from the psychological point of view; if we simply reflect on the feeling with which we look at the sins we have ourselves committed, and compare it with our feeling towards the sins of others, we shall, I think, only find a difference in so far as one or other of these feelings is vitiated by our own limitations of knowledge or errors of attitude.   In an ideal case, when we have struck the true balance between harshness and laxity of judgment, we feel to

our own sins exactly as we feel to those of any other
person. We do not feel sorry for our own sins and
indignant at other people's; the sorrow and the indignation are both present in each case. A good man's
feeling towards the sins of others is exactly the same
kind of emotion as that which he feels towards his own.
The fact that we call this feeling one of penitence when
it regards himself and one of forgiveness (or punishment)
when it regards others must not mislead us; for this
is merely an example of the distinction according to
circumstances of two emotions which when considered
in themselves are seen to be one and the same.

But, it may be asked, can we really abstract emotions
in this way from their circumstances? Is not any
emotion simply the attitude of a will towards a particular
event or reality? And if this is so, we are right in
defining emotions by reference to their circumstances;
because where circumstances differ there must be some
difference in the state of mind which they evoke. The
objection is perfectly sound; and our merely psychological argument must be reinforced by asking whether
the circumstances in the two cases really are different.
In the one case we have a good man's attitude towards
the actions of his own evil past; in the other, his
attitude towards another man who is doing evil now.
The difference of time is plainly unimportant; we
do not think differently of an action merely as it is
present or past. The real question is the difference of
person.

We must remember that, since a will is what it does,
we cannot maintain that this good man is in every sense
the same man who was bad. The bad will has been
swept out of existence and its place taken by a good
will; the man is, as we say, a new man; a new motive
force lives in him and directs his actions. This does
not mean that he is not "responsible" in his present
state for the actions of his past. It means, if we must
press the conclusion, not that he can shirk the responsi-

bility for his own actions, but that he is bound to accept the responsibility for those of others ; and this is no paradox if we rid the word of its legal associations and ask what moral meaning it can have. For to call a man responsible means that he ought to be punished, and the punishment, the sorrow, that a good man undergoes for his own sins he does certainly undergo for the sins of other men.

Thus God, who is perfectly good, must feel repentance for the sins of men ; he bears in his own person the punishment which is their due, and by the communication to them of the spirit of his own penitence he leads them to repent, and so in self-punishment to work their own redemption. The divine and human sides, the objective and subjective, completely coincide. What God does man also does, and what man feels, God feels also.

(b) All human redemption thus comes from God, and is the re-birth in man's will of the original divine penitence. But in this immediate communication to man of the spirit of God, mediation is not excluded. In one sense, all right acting and true knowing involves utterly unmediated communion of the soul with God. As Elisha lay upon the dead child, his mouth upon his mouth, and his eyes upon his eyes, and his hands upon his hands, till the child came to life again, so the soul is quickened by complete, immediate contact with God, every part at once with every part. But though we know God directly or not at all, we yet know him only as revealed to us through various channels of illumination and means of grace. The mystic who dwells alone with God is only a mystic through social influences and the stimulus of his surroundings, and in his union with the divine mind he is united no less with all the community of living spirits.

So repentance comes not only from God but through paths which in a sense we distinguish from the activity of God. Every truth is reached through some stimulus or instruction which comes from a source in the world around us ; and in the same way repentance reaches us through human channels, and we repent of our sins because we see others repent of them. This is human vicarious penitence ; others suffer for our sins, the suffering being not a mere " natural consequence " of the sin but specifically sorrow, penitence, that is, punishment for it ; and their suffering is literally the means of grace for us, the influence by which we come to our own repentance.

But this universal fact of human life is, like all others, summed up and expressed most completely in the divine manhood of the Christ. He alone is always and perfectly penitent ; for a sinful man cannot, while sinful, repent for his own sins or any others ; permanent penitence is only possible for a permanently sinless mind. And this repentance of Christ is not only subjectively complete, that is, unbroken by sins of his own, but objectively perfect also ; it is incapable of supplement or addition, sufficient to atone for the sins of the whole world, to convert all sinners by the spectacle of God's suffering. No further example could add anything to its force. There is only one way of destroying sin ; namely, to convert the sinner. And there is only one way of converting the sinner ; namely, to express to him, in such a way that he cannot but realise it, the attitude towards himself of a good will ; the attitude which unites condemnation and forgiveness in the concrete reality of vicarious repentance.

Thus the supreme example of sinless suffering is the salvation of the world ; final in the sense that nothing can be added to it, that every new repentance is identical with it ; not final, but only initial, in the sense that by itself it is nothing without the response it should awake, the infinite reproduction of itself in the consciousness of all mankind. It is not merely an example set up for our imitation ; not merely a guarantee of the possibilities of human life. It is an unfailing source and fountain of spiritual energy ; it gives to those who would imitate it the strength to work miracles, to cast aside their old selves and to enter upon a new life prepared from the beginning of the world ; for out of it power goes forth to draw all men to itself.

CHAPTER III

MIRACLE

There are three questions which may be asked about any supposed miraculous event. Did it happen? Why did it happen? and, Was it a miracle?

The first question is a matter for history to decide. No event can be proved or disproved to have happened except on historical grounds. The second question is also historical; for it lies with history to determine not only the actions of persons in the past, but also their motives. The remaining question, whether such and such an event was miraculous or not, is also in a sense historical, but (it might be said) less purely historical than the others. The philosophical assumption which underlies it is more evident than in the other cases. Every historical question involves such assumptions. The question "Did it happen?" implies the assumption that past facts are ascertainable; a technical point in the theory of knowledge. The question "Why was it done?" involves in the same way the ethical implication that people have motives for their actions. But these philosophical implications do not strike us when the historical questions are asked, because they are generally admitted and are not as a rule called in question.

But when we are asked, "Was it miraculous?" we at once feel the necessity for a philosophical inquiry before the question can be answered. Do miracles

happen? we ask in turn; and what do you mean by
a miracle? These questions form the starting-point of
the present chapter. We shall offer no opinion on the
historicity of any particular miracle, or on the motive
which may have underlain it; we shall confine ourselves strictly to the problem of defining the conception
of miracle as such. If this can be done, it will perhaps
be of some service to the historical theologian. At
present his work is much impeded by metaphysical
difficulties; by doubt as to what kind of evidence and
how much of it is necessary to establish the fact of a
miracle; by fear that if he pronounces against the
truth of a miraculous story he may be accused of
joining hands with the party which denies *a priori* the
existence of miracle, and that if he accepts such stories
at their face value, as he accepts other historical matter,
enlightened persons will denounce him for an obscur-
antist believer in the impossible.

1. These difficulties are due to the prevalence of a
theory, or definition, of miracle which it is our first
business to examine. It is certainly possible to define
miracle in such a way that the whole difficulty is
evaded. If we merely say "a miracle is something
striking, wonderful, awe-inspiring"—then no problem
arises; but such definitions will probably be suggested
only by persons to whom controversy has imparted the
wisdom of the serpent. And, covering as they do such
things as a Homeric simile or dawn on the Alps, they
are not accurate representations of the common
theological use of the word. They are rather criticisms of that usage, or confessions that it cannot be
maintained.

The definition which gives rise to our problem is to
the effect that a miraculous event is one caused by
God's interference with the course of nature. This is
the definition which we shall first examine; and we
shall then proceed to deal with the two bye-forms of it,
one, that a miracle is an event due to the intervention

of a higher natural law negating a lower one ; the other, that it represents God's departure from his normal modes of action. We shall treat these two later, because they are in essence modifications of the first definition, and only arise when the dualism inherent in the first has proved fatal to its defence.

This dualism may be expressed as follows. If we ask what is meant by " nature " in the above formula, we are told that it consists of a series of events such that any given event is the effect of that which went before it and the cause of that which follows. In the " order of nature" the precise character and occasion of every event is rigidly determined, A producing B ; B, C ; C, D-E-F. Now when a miracle happens, this series is broken. Instead of C leading to D, the divine will substitutes for D a new state of things, δ, which becomes the cause of subsequent events ; so that the sequence now runs ABC/$\delta\epsilon\zeta$. The new factor δ might, it is true, appear alongside of D, not instead of it ; but we generally regard a miracle as the cancelling of what was going to happen and the positive substitution of something else. Now δ is an event, a " physical " event just as C is ; and the dualism therefore consists in this, that a given physical event may be caused either naturally or miraculously. There are two different principles by which events are originated, existing side by side in complete independence.

The dislike of dualism as such is sometimes represented as nothing more than a curious idiosyncrasy of the philosophic mind ; either as a matter of taste, or as a weakness due to a desire to make the world look simpler than it really is. " Cheap and easy " are almost permanent epithets for the type of theory called monism, which explains reality as issuing from a single principle. And doubtless many monistic theories deserve such names ; for to construct a view of the universe by leaving out all the facts except one is both easy and cheap. But monism properly understood is

only another word for the fundamental axiom of all
thinking, namely that whatever exists stands in some
definite relation to the other things that exist.   And
the essence of dualism or pluralism is that it catalogues
the things that exist without sufficiently determining
these inter-relations.

Suppose, for instance, we discover the existence of
two principles A and B, and then go on to ask what is
the relation between them.   We may begin by saying
" I don't know " ; and that might be called provisional
pluralism, a necessary stage in the development of
any theory.   But we must add " I mean to find out if
I can " ; and that is to profess our faith in a monistic
solution.   For the principles A and B, connected by
the principle C, really form one principle ABC.   The
true pluralist, when asked for the relation between A
and B, would reply boldly " There isn't any " ; and that
is as meaningless as if we should describe two points
in space between which there was no distance.   This
could only mean that they were the same point ; and
similarly to say that there was no relation between A
and B is only sense if it means that there is no
difference between them, that they are the same
principle.

Thus our objection to the bare dualism of God and
nature is that it is not yet a theory at all ; it simply
sets the two principles before us without attempting
to show how they are related.   We want to know
the difference between them, and the nature of a whole
in which they can exist side by side.   This simply
amounts to saying that the dualism is a provisional one ;
and people who deal in such dualisms are often quite
ready to admit that the dualism is " not absolute."   It
might be thought hypercritical to reply that by such
an admission they confessed that they were trying to
secure the advantage of maintaining a theory while
knowing it to be unsound ; and we shall rather ask
whether, regarded simply as provisional, the dualism

does what it claims to do, and finds room for the complete reality of each side.

(*a*) On examination, it appears that justice is done to neither side by the attempt to regard them dualistically as parallel realities. A God who is not the source of all being is no true God ; and this defect is not removed by saying that God created and can interfere with nature. Even if this were so, even if every event in the present were the outcome of an original creative purpose, nature would still be something alien to, something essentially different from, the activity of God ; for the events by which God's original creation became the world as we now see it would be, by definition, naturally and not divinely caused. God, on this theory, created the world in the beginning ; once created, it continued to develop by its own impetus, which impetus cannot be called a divine law because it is precisely nature, the principle which the theory distinguished from God's activity. And therefore the world only expresses God's purpose remotely and obscurely ; his first act has been so overlaid by natural causation that the present world is in fact purely natural, not in itself divine at all.

The same defect appears in any given miracle ; for any such event is only a reproduction in miniature of the original miracle of creation. God's activity ceases the moment it is put forth ; at once it is seized upon and petrified by natural law into a part of the causal system. Nothing is God's but the bare abstract point of departure, his own subjective volition. He may interfere with nature as he likes, but nature remains essentially uninfluenced, for every interference is no sooner accomplished than the divinity vanishes from it and it becomes mere nature. God therefore is absolutely unexpressed in the world, however frequent his miracles may be ; for by the time they reach our senses they have lost all their miraculous character. He is reduced to an abstractly transcendent being, aloof from reality and eternally impotent either to influence it or to use it as the expression of his own nature. He is thus shorn of all true Godhead, and becomes little more than the spectator of an automatic world.

(*b*) But if God's reality is sacrificed by the dualistic conception, that of nature is preserved no better. Granting that God can suspend for a moment the operation of natural law, and substitute a different conclusion to a causal process, what are we to think of such laws? A miracle is described as an exception to a law of nature. But a law that admits exceptions is not a law at all. It explains nothing because it does not express a necessary connexion. A connexion that is at the mercy of any one, even of omnipotence, is simply not necessary, not a connexion, not an explanation. We are told, rightly or wrongly, that no law is certain, no rule free from exceptions ; but if we could accept that doctrine the only inference would be that the "natural order," the system of universal law, was non-existent. But this theory of miracle is based on assuming that a great proportion of events is really accounted for by laws of this kind. It assumes that there are events of which we can say : "It must be so because there is a universal law that it *is* so." If the supposed law is subject to exceptions, its position as a law is forfeited. It is not entitled to plead "an omnipotent will overrode my arbitrament" ; that would be merely a confession that it was not a law at all as the scientist understands laws.

There is a great deal of loose talking and vague thinking on this point. People speak of laws exactly as if they were individual persons ; we hear of the reign of law, the compulsion of law, the decree of law, or even sometimes of disobedience and defiance of the laws of nature. Such wild mythology obscures the true conception of law so hopelessly in the popular mind, that people can entertain the idea of two laws conflicting, or of a law being suspended or abrogated, as if these

laws of nature were rival legislators or the arbitrary acts
of a sovereign.   We must try to remember that a law
of nature is a statement of a universal fact, not a
command.   It cannot be "disobeyed," because it does
not tell any one to do anything; it can only be "broken"
in the sense that we can find instances in which it does
not hold good.   But if such instances do arise, the
universal statement is no longer a true one, it no longer
represents a fact; and we have to say, not " In this case
such and such a law is broken," but "This case proves
that such and such a statement or theory is not
universally true, and that the supposed law does not
exist, or requires modification so as to exclude cases of
this sort."   The kind of thought which imagines
natural law as subject to exceptions is precisely that of
the most unscientific and inadequate type; as if Newton
after observing the fall of the apple had written,
"Everything has a natural property of falling to the
earth ; this is why the apple falls.   Exceptions to this
law may be seen in smoke, kites, and the heavenly
bodies."

The reader may remember how we showed in a
former chapter that matter and mind cannot exist side
by side, since if any matter exists everything must be
material and therefore if any mind exists all must be
spiritual (Part II. Ch. II. § 1).   We have now discovered
a parallel or rather an identical truth ; natural laws
admitting exceptions are not natural laws at all, and
divine acts subject to natural conditions are not divine.
The fusion of God and nature which we called miracle
is a monstrosity, because the two principles are by their
very definition mutually exclusive, and neither can exist
if compelled to share the universe with the other.   We
must follow up the argument, taking each in turn as
the absolute principle, since it is now clear that we can
no longer defend our original dualism.

2. We must therefore posit either nature or God as
the sole reality.   We are seeking only for a basis for

the conception of miracle ; the general metaphysical question was worked out at length in Part II. Ch. II., and we need not repeat the arguments there employed.

(*a*) If we try to maintain that nature is the sole reality, and rebuild our conception of miracle on that basis, we shall have to define the miraculous as the case where one law of nature is overridden by another ; the " emergence of a higher law " or some such phrase is used to cover theories of this kind. It is not difficult to see where the fallacy lies. In inductive logic we are told that a higher law explains a lower, the lower being an instance of the operation of a higher. In this sense of lower and higher, the higher is the more universal; the laws of the conic section explain those of the circle because they are higher in the sense that the circle is one kind, and only one kind, of conic section. Now if in this sense of the word we were told that a higher law overrode a lower, we should reply that the phrase is a contradiction in terms ; the lower law is simply one instance of the higher, and to talk of a law overriding one of its own instances is meaningless. The fact that two men and two women are four people is an instance of the more general fact that twice two is four ; it is inconceivable that the higher or more general fact, twice two is four, should " override " the lower or less general so as to make two men and two women into three people.

There is only one sense in which one law can conflict with or override another ; that is, when the " laws " involved are not laws of nature but acts of will. If nurse makes a law that baby goes to bed at six, that law may be overridden by superior authority ; there may be a parental law that baby stays up later on birthdays. " Higher " in this case has quite a different sense ; it means " promulgated by a higher authority." And " law " in this case means not a law of nature, the statement of a universal fact, but a command given by one will to another.

The overridden law, in short, cannot be a natural law, because such laws, being simply general truths, cannot be overridden ; nor can the higher law be a law of nature miraculously overriding the decision of a will, because a real law of nature in conflict with a will would win every time, not in miraculous cases only. Therefore if we define miracle as the outcome of a conflict between two laws, neither law can be regarded as a law of nature ; each is an act of will, and the higher law is the act of the more potent will.

The result of defining miracle by reference to the conception of natural law is that it compels us to describe nature in terms only applicable to spirit. The attempt to combine the two conceptions, miracle and nature, leads to the explicit reversal of the very definition of nature.

(*b*) We have now to examine the third of our original definitions, namely that which escapes the dualism of God and nature by resting on the single conception of God. We shall then regard miracle as one kind of divine operation, distinguished from another kind, the non-miraculous, by some criterion to be further determined. Two such criteria may be suggested: (i.) that of normal and abnormal, (ii.) that of mediate and immediate.

(i.) The distinction between normal and abnormal action presupposes the idea of a norm, a principle or rule generally followed, but not invariably adhered to ; admitting of exceptions but only in exceptional circumstances. Such rules are conceived as made by mind for mind ; they are not necessities to which the will is subject, but forms of its own activity. They are familiar enough in our own life; and it is assumed that they exist no less in that of God. Now when man makes himself rules, he breaks them in one of two ways. Either his original purpose fails him through weakness, caprice, or sinfulness ; or else he abandons it because unforeseen circumstances have arisen which make it impossible or wrong to pursue his intention. These are the causes of human abnormality ; defect in the man or defect in the rule.   Neither cause can be operative in the case of God.   He is not vacillating and infirm of purpose ; and he is not subject to the occurrence of events whose possibility he had overlooked.   No reason, in fact, can ever arise why God should ever depart from his own rules of conduct.

The conception of a rule or norm thus leads not to the explanation but to the denial of miracle.   Abnormality implies that either the rule or the exception was wrong ; alternatives equally impossible to the divine wisdom.

And this argument is often used against those who uphold the possibility of miracles.   But we are not concerned to prove their possibility or impossibility; we are seeking only for a definition of what the word means. Consequently we cannot end our inquiry here ; if it is said that the abnormal never happens in God we must ask whether the conception of normality is sound ; whether it is true to say that God always acts in perfect conformity to perfect principles.   The doctrine as stated appears simple and unobjectionable, but it is in fact either tautologous or misleading.   In the first place, principles of conduct as known to ourselves are, if perfectly universal, always perfectly empty.   They give no information as to what you are to do on any particular occasion.   "Always do right " ; "Always treat others as ends in themselves " ;   "Render to every man his due " ; these are absolutely universal ; they apply to every case of conduct you can imagine.   But they are also alike in not prescribing any definite course of action whatever.   No doubt in a certain case the maxim "Always do right" acquires a content from the fact that there is only one right thing to do ; therefore, the principle " Always do right " appears in this given case to mean "Confess your fault and take your punishment," or the like.   But this content is not supplied by the general principle itself ; it is supplied by the answer to the question stimulated by that principle : " What *is* right ? " A person who did not know how to behave on a given occasion would not be helped by the principle unless he intended to act capriciously ; in that case it might remind him that he had duties. But one may safely say that a conscientious person never thinks of the principle as a principle ; and if his attention was called to it, he would say that it told him nothing he wanted to know. In a sense, he acts on it : but it does not explain why he did *this* and not *that*.

The truly universal rule, then, is absolutely empty. It is doubtless true to say God always acts on it, but to say that adds nothing to our knowledge of God. It does not let us into the secret of his will. It merely staves off our inquiry with a truism ; as if one should say that the secret of good painting was always to put the right colour in the right place. True, no doubt ; but not very helpful.

There is another type of rule which represents an attempt to overcome this difficulty by supplying a content. It definitely tells you what you are to do and what you are not to do ; whether simply because agreement on such points is convenient for social purposes (keep to the right, or, last boy in bed put out the gas) or because every case of the rule represents a definite and binding moral duty (thou shalt do no murder ; *audi alteram partem* ; always protect a lady). Since the first type, the absolutely universal, has proved useless, this must be the kind of rule which the theory has in mind ; and the doctrine must be that there is (if only we could formulate it) a complete body of such rules which, taken altogether, cover the whole of life and provide for every case ; that a breach of one is either a crime or the sign of the law's imperfection ; and that therefore the rules of conduct laid down for himself by God are never broken at all. Such a body of rules constitutes what is generally called a casuistry ; not using the word in a bad sense, but in the strict and accurate sense in which it signifies the normative science of conduct, the complex of rules defining one's duty in any given situation. For man, according to the doctrine we are examining, casuistry is always imperfect because of his deficient imagination of possible emergencies, and on account of the differences between man and man which make it impossible for all to be guided by quite the same principles. For God these difficulties disappear and the science would be perfect.

Now there are two points about the essential nature of this science which must be observed. (*a*) First, obeying its rules is not the same thing as doing a moral action. If I am asked "Why did you do that?" I may reply either "Because the rule says I must," or else "Because I felt I ought." (I do not assert that there are no other possible answers.) But these are quite different answers and represent two different points of view. The first answer does no doubt suggest the question "But why obey the rules?" and to that the reply may be "Well, I suppose one *ought* to obey them"; but as a matter of fact this ulterior question has, in most cases, not been raised at all, and obeying the rule as such has no further moral implication, or at most a vague and distant one. The two answers may coincide; but in that case the first is not felt to be of any importance. "I ought" stands by itself and gains nothing by the addition "I am told to." In conduct the only thing that confers moral value is motive; and if one is conscious of no motive except obedience to a rule, one cannot claim the action as a moral one. Whereas if one is conscious of the action as a duty, its legality no longer makes any difference. To obey a rule may be socially indispensable; it may be educative; it may be prudent; but it is not a free, morally initiated action. Morality knows no rules; and the same is the case with art, and all spiritual activity.

But, it may be asked, are we to abolish all rules of conduct? What would become of the world if we did?

That is exactly the point. The world, taken at any given moment, requires education, it requires discipline; it is not by any means perfect or moral or self-dependent. We were not proposing to abolish laws and empirical maxims from our makeshift society. We merely assert that for a perfectly moral being, one who really apprehended duty as such, these maxims and laws would recede into the background and disappear ; such a being simply ignores and does not act on them at all, but acts merely on his intuition of duty.

(β) The second point is that such rules contain an element of approximation and vagueness which can never be eliminated and therefore makes them unfit to serve as guides for a perfect intelligence. They are based on the supposition that cases and actions can be classified in such a way that the classification will provide the basis for a distinction between right and wrong : and this supposition is fallacious.

These rules are always general, by their very nature; they lay down that an action of the type A is always right, an action of the type B always wrong. On inspection, however, it proves impossible to find any class of actions of which we can say that it is always right or always wrong, unless we have defined it in such a way as to beg the question. Thus, " never tell a lie " is a good rule ; but telling a lie is by no means always wrong. The least imaginative person could think of a situation in which it was a positive duty. On the other hand, " commit no murder " is absolutely valid only because murder means *wrongful* killing ; so that the rule is a tautology.

But further : actions cannot strictly be classified at all. What is a lie? Intentional deceit? Then it covers such cases as ambiguous answers, refusals to answer, evasions ; or even the mere withholding of information when none has been demanded ; and we cannot easily say when such concealment of the truth is intentional. To lay a trap for an opponent in controversy would probably have to be called lying, as well as countless other cases in which we do not use the word. A classification of actions, in short, can only exist so long as we refrain from asking the precise meaning of the terms employed.

Therefore a system of casuistry is not only useless but actually impossible for a really moral mind ; it is essentially a makeshift, vanishing with the advance in spiritual life. This is not because our rules are bad rules ; it follows from their mere nature *as* rules. The nearer we come to true living, the more we leave behind not bad rules merely, but all rules. Thus Beethoven said that the rules were all his very humble servants ; and it is true that the rules formulated by his masters met with little respect at his hands. But that (it may be argued) was because they were bad, imperfect, inadequate rules; he created rules of his own, and those he did obey. For instance, he altered sonata-form a great deal ; but he did write sonatas. Musical scholars tell us that John Sebastian Bach did not write fugues ; and that is true if by fugues you mean compositions of an arbitrarily rigid and academic type. But he did write Bachesque fugues, or whatever you please to call them ; he did write one definite type of composition, and Beethoven wrote another type. Thus each made his own rules. They were not the rules his masters taught him ; but the rules he made he kept.

No, we must reply, he did not. The form of the Beethoven sonata varies between Op. 2 and Op. 111 so vastly that we cannot lay down any one set of regulations and say "These are Beethoven's sonata-rules." No doubt if we take few enough rules and sufficiently abstract ones, we can arrive at some that Beethoven never broke ; but if you had pointed out the fact to him, he would probably have taken care to break them all in his next sonata. The fact is that the conception of rule to which we are now appealing is a fluid conception ; a Beethoven can abandon his old rules at pleasure and take a leap into a new world, guided only by the spirit of music itself.   What then are Beethoven's rules of composition?   Here is the secret : they are recast for every new work.   The "rule" is nothing but another name for the ground-plan of the new work itself.   He simply invents new rules as he goes along, to meet his requirements.   And that means that in the sense of the word with which we started he has no rules at all.

Thus in a sense every action obeys a law.   But the law is newly shaped for every fresh action ; in fact, it simply is the action.   Therefore the original theory, that there were certain rules established by himself eternally which God in virtue of his own consistency was bound to obey, is seen to be a delusion.   We cannot escape the analogy by saying that Beethoven's development was a continual improvement of existing laws, and that such an improvement is inconceivable in God ; for Haydn's rules were quite as good as Beethoven's for the work they had to do, and Beethoven's early rules are no worse in themselves than his later ones.   Then why did he change them ?   Simply because one rule is only applicable to one case ; and to apply it to another case is pedantry.

If we cannot speak of a rule fixing the normal treatment of every case, neither can we speak of a single dominant purpose which determines how every action shall be done.   This would be only another form of the same fallacy.   I may, owing to my obsession by a dominant purpose, be led to treat people in the lump, abstractly, and not as real individuals ; I may ignore the finer shades of difference and lose my sense of proportion.   But in such a case the purpose is a bad one, in that it has a bad effect on my conduct ; or at least I am the wrong person to carry it out.   To suppose that God acts on immutable rules because he has an immutable purpose is a mere confusion of terms.   His immutable purpose might surely be to do justice in every separate case and to avoid all the abstract mechanism of immutable rules.

We cannot base miracle on the distinction between normal and abnormal cases ; because the distinction is not to be found in God. Where everything is perfectly individual, the class or norm no longer has a meaning ; the individual is a law to itself. Relatively, this is true for man in proportion as he approximates to perfection ; it is absolutely true of God.

(ii.) The second attempt to reintroduce the notion of miracle on the basis of God's sole reality was the distinction between mediate and immediate action on the part of God. This again—I hope the subdivision is not becoming wearisome—will take two forms according as God's " medium " is man (including other spirits) or nature.

(*a*) That God acts either directly or through natural processes is precisely the dualistic conception which we found wanting at the outset ; so we can pass on at once.

(β) God's action is now considered as either direct, or mediated through the agency of man. I do not wish to spend time over the conception of mediacy ; we have already examined it in another chapter, and the only question here is whether it fits the notion of miracle. Plainly it does not. If God delegates power to a creature, and that creature then operates of itself, the action is mediate ; whereas God's delegation itself or his subsequent interference is immediate. But the distinction is too arbitrary to require serious refutation. In the Gospels, Jesus works miracles ; in the Acts, the Apostles. No doubt the power comes from God, often in answer to direct prayer. But if God's power is not mediate when it is seen in the person of Peter or Paul, what does the word mean ? It must surely be held that the power to work miracles is no less mediate than the other powers which God bestows upon his creatures.

3. Of all these forms in which the definition of miracle appears we have discovered that every one is

P

based upon some error, some dualism which is a mere metaphysical fiction and has no existence in reality. No dualism is ultimate, and no dualism that is not ultimate is a suitable basis for a theological system. It stands self-confessed a foundation of sand. We must declare frankly that the common conception of miracle is untenable. It is a hybrid conception, compounded of two conflicting and absolutely irreconcilable views ; one atheistic, the other theistic ; one material, the other spiritual ; one false, the other true.

(*a*) But we must maintain that we have not forfeited anything of value. Instead of finding the operation of God in isolated and controvertible facts, we are now free to find it universalised in everything that is true or good or beautiful. And so far from admitting, as some persons pretend, that between elevating all these things to the rank of God and depressing them all to the rank of matter there is little to choose, we must assert that the former view alone does justice to the facts of common consciousness as well as to the truths of philosophy.

For up to now we have refrained from asking for a working limitation of the use of the term miracle. If now we ask what is and what is not called miraculous, the difficulty of making a distinction will be very evident. Thus, excluding merely superstitious interpretations of Transubstantiation, would a normal Christian describe the Real Presence in the Eucharist as miraculous? If so, then is not the equally real presence in prayer a miracle ? And then what of the real presence which surrounds the religious man in every moment of his life ? To a religious person it is surely true to say that nothing exists that is not miraculous. And if by miracle he means an act of God realised as such, he is surely justified in finding miracles everywhere. If the Real Presence is not a miracle, then what is ? An act of healing ? But are we really prepared to maintain that healing done by non-medical means is miraculous, as distinguished from medical healing which is not ? If miraculous means mysterious (as in common speech it often does) we can draw no such distinction. We are not in a position to say that while a headache cured by prayer is a mystery and therefore presumably miraculous, a headache cured by drugs is scientifically understood and therefore not mysterious nor miraculous. For our criticism of causation has shown us that we do not " understand " the operation of the drug in the least, and are therefore not entitled to call it either miraculous or the reverse, whereas we must for ever call it mysterious. Every cure is equally a miracle, and every doctor (like every other active and creative mind) a miracle-worker, in the only sense which can reasonably be attached to the word.

For again, if the miraculous and the non-miraculous must be distinguished, into which category does human life and activity fall ? That again cannot be answered. It is not nature in the sense required ; it must be miracle, and yet we do not call it so. And if our scheme of reality is such that we can find no place in it for man, what is to become of it as a philosophy ?

(b) But, even after reconciling ourselves to the fact that all events are volitions and that the mechanically controlled " order of nature " is non-existent, we may still ask, Does not this view overthrow all we have believed about the uniformity of nature ? And if we give up the uniformity of nature, where is our boasted volition ? for without a reliable and steadygoing nature to ride upon, Will would never be able to get to the end of its journey.

(i.) Whether it overthrows our beliefs depends, perhaps, on how far they are true. What do we mean by uniformity ? That A always produces a. But A and a, definite events, only happen once each ; uniformity has no place there. Very well ; we mean that events of the class A always produce (or rather precede) events of the class a. The class A consists of B, C, D, all alike ; the class a of β, γ, δ, all similarly alike. Then an event in the first class will always precede one in the second. Produce, we cannot say ; that would be to claim a knowledge of their inner connexion which we do not possess. Then all it comes to is this, that there are resemblances between events, and that if events B, C, D, are like one another, their contexts β, γ, δ, will also show resemblances. That is what we describe as the uniformity of nature. The so-called classes are only our way of recording these resemblances. But in resemblance there is nothing alien to mind as such. Beethoven's sonatas resemble one another ; so do Napoleon's battles and Shakspere's sonnets. Uniformity is a perfectly obvious characteristic of the products of mind. To argue from resemblance to determinism is not uncommon ; but it is totally fallacious.

If recurrence or resemblance proved determinism, the same conclusion is equally proved by any single event. There is nothing in recurrence that is not already present in the single instance. Indeed some determinists have argued that because a certain man once did a certain action, therefore he was bound to do it. This seems a *reductio ad absurdum* ; and yet if we can argue from frequency to necessity, the question " How often must a thing happen before you know it was bound to happen?" can have only one answer :—" Once is enough." All the arguments, therefore, by which we prove that matter is mechanical in its behaviour will prove the same of mind ; and the uniformity of nature differs not at all in character from the uniformity of spirit.

(ii.) Granted—and by now we seem bound to grant —that a ball, let drop, falls in virtue not of an inexorable law but of a volition, and that the volition might will otherwise, we may still say that the possibility of a ball's thus changing its habits need not seriously disturb our practical calculations. We have to deal not only with things, but with men ; and if the engineer feels justified in calculating the strength of his materials on a basis of absolute uniformity, the organiser of labour is no less ready to calculate the average output of a workman and to act on his calculations. If we try to carry the principle of uniformity too far, it will fail us whether our assumption is that any man will write an equally good epic or that any steel will make an equally good razor. In practice, we learn to discriminate ; we distinguish between the things that any man can do and the things for which an exceptional man is needed ; and in exactly the same way we learn how far it is safe to reckon on the uniformity of matter and at what point we must begin to look for diversity.

Uniformity, in a word, is relative to our needs; and to suggest that a game of cricket, for instance, would be impossible if we supposed that the ball might suddenly decide to fly to the moon, is no less and no more sensible than to suggest that it is impossible because the bowler might put it in his pocket and walk off the field. We know that the friend we trust is abstractly capable, if he wished, of betraying us, but that does not prevent our trusting him. It may be that our faith in the uniformity of matter is less removed from such a trust than we sometimes imagine. Whether we describe it as faith in matter or faith in God makes, after all we have said, little difference.

But if we mean by uniformity the mere statement that things behave alike and that we can rely on them to do so, it is only one side of the truth and, perhaps, not the most important side. To see uniformities is the mark of a superficial observer ; to demand uniformities is characteristic of all the less vital and more mechanical activities. What we call uniformity in people, in society and history, is generally a name for our own lack of insight ; everything looks alike to the person who cannot see differences. What we demand of a friend is not constancy alone; it is resourcefulness, adaptability, variety ; a continual readjustment to the new demands of an always new intercourse. To the eye of perfect insight, nothing is merely uniform ; everything is unique. For such a consciousness there are no classes, there are only individuals ; not in chaos, for every individual is related to every other :—

> All things, by immortal power,
> Near or far,
> Hiddenly
> To each other linkèd are,
> That thou canst not stir a flower
> Without troubling of a star.[1]

The true relation between individuals is not the resemblance which connects members of a class, but the co-operation which unites parts of a whole. Such parts are not bound by abstract rules. They are free, but their freedom is not caprice, for they act in and through the whole and each other, so that the whole perpetually re-creates itself in their actions.

If materialism only means the mood in which we have tired of the infinity and intimacy of the real, and lapse wearily into a ghost-land of our own, peopled by abstractions which we can command if we cannot enjoy them, the only hope is in some sudden inrush of life, something to startle us into consciousness once more and to scatter the ghosts by the blaze of its own light. This is the function of those events which we call, *par excellence*, Miracles ; they force themselves upon our eyes as a standing testimony to the deadness and falsity of our materialistic dogmas, and compel us to face reality as it is, free, infinite, self-creative in unpredicted ways. But the very meaning and purpose of miracle is lost if we regard it as unique and exclusive ; if we set up for our superstitious worship, side by side with the true God, an idol of man's making, adored under the name of Nature.

---

[1] F. Thompson, *The Mistress of Vision.*

INDEX

215

Printed by R. & R. CLARK, LIMITED, *Edinburgh.*

KEY TEXTS

Classic Works in the History of Ideas

Also Available in this series:

ARISTOTELIANISM
John Leofric Stocks
ISBN 1 85506 222 4 : 1925 Edition : 174pp : £12.99/$19.95

DESCARTES
Anthony Kenny
ISBN 1 85506 236 4 : 1968 Edition : 256pp : £9.99/$14.95

AN ESSAY ON PHILOSOPHICAL METHOD
R. G. Collingwood
ISBN 1 85506 392 1 : 1933 Edition : 240pp : £14.99/$24.95

FOUR DISSERTATIONS
David Hume
New Introduction by John Immerwahr
ISBN 1 85506 393 X : 1757 Edition : 258pp : £14.99/$24.95

THE HUNTING OF LEVIATHAN
Samuel Mintz
ISBN 1 85506 481 2 : 1962 Edition : 200pp : £14.99/$24.95

AN INTRODUCTION TO THE PHILOSOPHY OF HISTORY
W. H. Walsh
ISBN 1 85506 170 8 : 1961 Edition : 176pp : £12.99/$19.95

OUTLINES OF A PHILOSOPHY OF ART
R. G. Collingwood
ISBN 1 85506 316 6 : 1925 Edition : 110pp : £10.99/$18.95

PHILOSOPHICAL STUDIES
J. McT. E. McTaggart (Edited with an original introduction by S. V. Keeling)
New Introduction by Gerald Rochelle
ISBN 1 85506 479 0 : 1934 Edition : 300pp : £12.99/$19.95

THE PHILOSOPHY OF RELIGION 1875–1980
Alan P. F. Sell
ISBN 1 85506 482 0 : 1988 Edition : 260pp : £12.99/$19.95

THE REASONABLENESS OF CHRISTIANITY
John Locke
New Introduction by Victor Nuovo
ISBN 1 85506 522 3 : 1794 Edition : 440pp : £17.99/$29.95

SCHOPENHAUER
Patrick Gardiner
ISBN 1 85506 525 8 : 1963 Edition : 315pp : £14.99/$24.95

SIX SECULAR PHILOSOPHERS
Lewis White Beck
ISBN 1 85506 518 5 : 1960 Edition : 126pp : £9.99/$15.95

SOME DOGMAS OF RELIGION
J. McT. E. McTaggart
New Introduction by Gerald Rochelle
ISBN 1 85506 519 3 : 1930 Edition : 299pp : £13.99/$24.95

THOMAS HOBBES
A. E. Taylor
ISBN 1 85506 523 1 : 1908 Edition : 136pp : £9.99/$14.95

THE UNCONSCIOUS. A CONCEPTUAL ANALYSIS
Alasdair MacIntyre
ISBN 1 85506 520 7 : 1958 Edition : 109pp : £11.99/$19.95

UK Office
11 Great George Street, Bristol BS1 5RR
Tel. (0117) 929 1377, Fax (0117) 922 1918

USA Office
Books International, P.O. Box 605, Herndon, Virginia 22070, USA
Tel. 1-703-435-7064, Fax 1-703-689-0660